Setting up and Running
a Limited Company

Setting up and Running a Limited Company

A comprehensive guide to forming and operating a company as a director and shareholder

ROBERT BROWNING
4th edition

howtobooks

Published by How to Books Ltd,
3 Newtec Place, Magdalen Road,
Oxford OX4 1RE, United Kingdom
Tel: 01865 793806   Fax: 01865 248780
email: info@howtobooks.co.uk
www.howtobooks.co.uk

Second edition 1999
Reprinted 1999
Third edition 2001
Fourth edition 2003

British Library Cataloguing in Publication Data.
A catalogue record for this book is available from
the British Library.

Cover design by Baseline Arts Ltd, Oxford
Produced for How To Books by Deer Park Productions
Typeset by Anneset, Weston-super-Mare, Somerset
Printed and bound by Cromwell Press, Trowbridge, Wiltshire

NOTE: The material contained in this book is set out in good
faith for general guidance and no liability can be accepted
for loss or expense incurred as a result of relying in particular
circumstances on statements made in the book. Laws and
regulations are complex and liable to change, and readers should
check the current position with the relevant authorities before
making personal arrangements.

Contents

List of Illustrations

Preface

to the fourth edition

Businesses are all around you. Every time you go to the shops, the pub, the dentist or the petrol service station you are dealing with a business. While all those businesses serve you with the goods and services you want, it is normally of little consequence to you how each business is run.

Things are very different if it is your business. It is as well to know what you are getting yourself into when you start. Most lessons in life are learned the hard way. This is how you get your experience but this book is intended to help you understand the mechanics of running a business through a limited company. The aim is also to save you from as many mistakes as possible.

Remember good judgement comes from experience but experience comes from poor judgement!

You may have already started your enterprise or you may just be embarking on it but everyone can learn from others. There are many pitfalls in business life and if you can cut down or eliminate them your worries will be far less.

All businesses need a framework within which to operate but the formation of a limited company must be done for the right reasons. A lot of businesses are run through companies but there are many legal implications attached to this.

New businesses and old sometimes fail but the existence of a company will not necessarily help in those circumstances. Limited liability is not a panacea for all ills. It represents a responsibility to the general public and gives business dealings a public face. Directors, too, have onerous responsibilities.

As a chartered accountant formerly in public practice with many years' experience of small businesses, I have tried to set out simply how to decide whether a company is right for you and, if so, how to go about it.

Apart from a detailed explanation of how to form and operate a company this book covers the filing of statutory information, your rights and responsibilities, the opening of bank accounts, keeping records, taxation, wages and salaries, marketing and auditing.

I would like to thank Alpha Searches Ltd., The Registrar of Companies, the Inland Revenue and Barclays Bank plc for the use of their forms and documentation and Messrs Baker Tilly, Chartered Accountants, for help in the original research of this book.

The text contains case studies and any names used in these or the rest of the book are purely fictitious. Any similarity between the names and those of real persons is purely coincidental.

Good luck with your enterprise. As you know, your country needs you.

Robert Browning

$$\bigodot 1$$

Deciding What You Want to Do

This book is about running your business through a limited company but first you must be clear about what you need to do. This initial chapter will help you decide this. It covers:

◆ starting in business

◆ being a sole trader or going into partnership

◆ buying a business

◆ getting professional help

◆ having a company or not.

STARTING IN BUSINESS

So you're going into business. You are going to become one of those entrepreneurs with a Rolls Royce and an expense account.

If only it were that easy. You have many decisions to take before you take the plunge into business.

Being in business

If you are engaged in an occupation, work or trade, whether commercial, industrial or professional, which includes the buying and selling of services then you are in business. Note that there is no mention of the word profit. Of course you would not be in business if you were not going to make a profit but it is not compulsory, just advisable.

This book is not intended to help you set up a business. It assumes you already have a product or service that you wish to sell or trade in. This book is designed to help you administer the business you have set up.

Owning your business

Asking who owns your business may seem a silly question but there can easily be other people involved. Your spouse or partner or son or daughter may work in the business or someone may have lent you some money to start it up. You must make sure that you know precisely the relationship any of these people have with you in your enterprise so that their interest can be properly taken into account.

Problems in business invariably arise through sloppy arrangements about money, so be advised to clarify these at the start.

Naming your business

There are a number of factors to take into account when deciding what to call your business. These are more fully discussed in Chapter 6, but you must choose a suitable name as this is what the public will refer to when talking about your business.

Defining your business

It is as well to define precisely what product or service your business is going to supply. Not only must you be able to inform your potential customers what you do but you must also be able to market and advertise your wares simply but succinctly. You must make it easy for your customer to deal with you.

BEING A SOLE TRADER OR GOING INTO PARTNERSHIP

Creating your set-up

You have established that you have a business with a name and a product or service to sell. You know who the owner is. You must now consider the implications of this. You have to decide what legal form your business will take. You can be a:

- sole trader
- partnership.

Being a sole trader
The word sole in this context means alone or the one and only. In business terms a sole trader is where the proprietor is the sole owner of a business although he or she may have employees.

Being a partnership
A partnership is defined by law in the Partnership Act 1890. It is the relationship which subsists between persons carrying on a business in common with a view to profit.

Put another way it is the relationship between people who have agreed to share the profits of a business carried on by all or any of them on behalf of all of them.

It might be advantageous to examine a little history. In the Middle Ages, when trading was growing fast, the individual traders found considerable advantage in combining with each other to carry on their business. The advantage was that it enabled them to command greater amounts of capital money they could not individually bring together and it helped them to combine and share their common experience and their profits. This was the beginning of partnerships.

Now if you have an arrangement to share the profits of your business with another person, the chances are that you are in partnership, sometimes known as a 'firm'. This may be a close friend with whom you have a rapport and would work well or someone who may have put money into your business. There is now, under the Limited Liability Partnerships Act 2000 the opportunity to form a partnership with limited liability. It must be registered with the Registrar of Companies and two of the partners called 'designated members' must accept responsibility for sending information to Companies House. This form of partnership is treated for tax purposes like any other.

BUYING A BUSINESS

While thinking of going into business it may have occurred to you that it might be simpler to buy a ready made business. After all, the hard slog of building up your customer base would be eliminated. The premises would already exist. There may be some staff and the stock may already be in the warehouse.

Don't be misled.

Why is the owner selling? Have you the money to compensate the owner for building it up? Suppose you pay too much.

If you are thinking of buying a business to make life easy, think again. Being in business is about **responsibility**.

There is no easy way to establishing your own business.

Seven steps to making your decision

Here is a simple guide to what you should consider when buying a business.

1. If you are already in business what are you looking to add?
   - Have you money to invest?
   - Have you expertise that can be employed in the additional business?

2. Define the business profile you would like to acquire.
   - Why will you be successful?
   - What size business are you looking for?
   - Where should it be located?

3. Learn about your market and do the research.
   - What are the growth areas?
   - What are the products you expect to sell?

4. What are the sources of businesses for sale?
   - Where will you find businesses advertised for sale?
   - What are the newspapers, magazines, business transfer agents and trade organisations which can help?
   - Sift through them carefully and investigate the ones that match your profile.
   - Consider suitable businesses which fit your profile but where the owner may not have decided to sell.

5. What effect will you have on the business if you buy it?
   - Will you be able to run it?
   - Have you the necessary knowledge of the business or the management skills?
   - Will you increase the profitability?
   - What changes will you make?

6. What is the maximum price you are prepared to pay?
   - Have you got up to date copies of the accounts of the business?
   - What are the profits?
   - How much money is invested in the business and is the return on capital good enough?
   - What are the debts and liabilities and have any been outstanding for a long time?

7. Are you ready to negotiate?
   - Have you got your facts prepared?
   - Are you ready to make a decision?

These questions are by no means exhaustive but they give you an idea of the things you should be considering before you put your money into a new venture.

Summary

1. Don't be tempted to pay too much for the business because you think it will give you a flying start.

2. Make sure you are entering a marketplace you can compete in.

3. Clarify the business you want to be in including its size, location and potential.

4. Be realistic about the effect of a change of ownership.

5. Question everything.

6. Crystallise your negotiating position. Know your top price and the one you are prepared to start at and stick to them. There is no such thing as a right price.

7. Obtain all the help you can from independent professional advisers (accountants, bankers, solicitors, surveyors, *etc*).

GETTING PROFESSIONAL HELP

Too many people either think they know it all or trust to luck when it comes to business matters. But even the most successful entrepreneur will tell you that they are always ready to listen to sound advice. The problem is how do you know it is sound. That comes with experience.

It is best to seek out the right **professional advisers** as early in your planning as possible. They may come up with advice which can materially affect the way your business operates and you can incorporate it before the process gets too far. It is important to avoid errors and misjudgments before they happen and unless this is done you may start your business with a permanent handicap.

Business advice can be obtained from:

◆ accountants
◆ bankers
◆ designers
◆ financial planners

- solicitors
- surveyors and estate agents.

Here are some points to watch.

Accountants

The term accountant does not necessarily mean they have any formal qualification. But you would be well advised to find an accountant who is a member of a recognised association as you will have some guarantee that he has followed a course of training and passed examinations in the skills required. The main bodies are:

- The Institute of Chartered Accountants in England & Wales (with FCA or ACA after their name)
- The Institute of Chartered Accountants of Scotland (CA)
- The Chartered Association of Certified Accountants (FCCA or ACCA)
- The Institute of Management Consultants (FIMA or AIMA) who deal mainly in management consultancy work as their name implies.

The cost should be discussed and agreed before any work is carried out.

Bankers

Banks offer a wide range of services including current accounts, loans and assistance with imports and exports. A particular bank can be chosen for a number of reasons, for example convenience, knowledge of the staff or even to separate your business accounts from your personal affairs. Larger branches have more discretionary powers as they do not have to pass decisions up to regional managers for approval but these would only be used when substantial funds are required.

Shop around to find what it will cost to run your account.

Designers

A good designer may be worth more than appears on the surface. The image of your product or the fitting out of your premises are important in giving your customers a feel for your business. This also applies to what your employees wear or what your stationery looks like. An impressive corporate image will always stand you in good stead.

Financial planners

They may help you in your marketing strategy, your budget projections, your organisation or the amount of money you may need to get your business off the ground. It is difficult to choose one but most large accountancy practices have specialist sections. You will normally be charged a flat fee based on your requirements.

Solicitors

A solicitor will be particularly useful in advising on the legal form of your business, the formation of your company, any contracts you may enter into and registration of patents and product protection. Costs vary but a solicitor will normally give you an estimate and some may give you a package deal. Fees must be 'fair and reasonable' by law.

Solicitors also specialise so make sure you get one who can deal with your needs. The larger the firm the bigger the range of activities they are likely to cover.

Surveyors and estate agents

Any transactions involving land or buildings will need the expertise of a surveyor to assure you that you are not entering into a contract unwisely. Matters covered include:

- surveys of premises
- planning permissions or change of the use of premises
- rates and rateable values
- whether the title is leasehold or freehold
- repairs and maintenance clauses in agreements.

The recognised body is The Royal Institution of Chartered Surveyors (FRICS or ARICS) and if you are involved in the valuations you could use the services of a member of the Incorporated Society of Valuers and Auctioneers.

Costs are again a matter of negotiation and agreement.

With all the above professional advisers do not hesitate to take out references or seek advice from people you know who use them. Personal recommendations from friends and colleagues are usually sound.

HAVING A COMPANY OR NOT

You now have to decide whether you want to trade through a company or not. Like life itself there are advantages and disadvantages in everything but the decision has to be taken. Nothing is irrevocable but remember there is always a cost. It is far better to weigh up the pros and cons first.

How the company was born

Look at a little history again.

When trade increased dramatically in the 19th century traders began to get together and run their businesses jointly. However, the increased activity also increased the burdens on individual partners. The property and debts of the firm were considered to be the property and debts of the individual partners. Therefore partnerships had no legal existence apart from the individual partners.

Then in 1844 an Act of Parliament was passed for the Registration of Joint Stock Companies and such an incorporated company could now hold property, incur debts and sue and be sued in its own name. The members (or partners) were no longer responsible for such matters individually. This was known as limited liability.

Differences between a company and a partnership or sole trader

Some of the differences are:

	Partnership or sole trader	*Company*
Members' liability	Unlimited	Limited
Number of members	Limited	Unlimited
Transfer of interest	Only with consent of other partners	Shares may be transferred
Capital introduced	By arrangement with other partners	Fixed by company rules
Profit sharing	-ditto-	-ditto-

Advantages of a company and of a partnership

Advantages of a company

1. A company has limited liability and it does not extend to the separate assets of each member whereas a partner's liabilities are not limited and extend, if necessary, to the whole of their individual estates.

2. The shares of a company are easily transferred but the value of the interest of a partner is much more difficult to determine.

3. The death of a company member does not affect the existence of a company. If a partner dies, however, the partnership ceases to exist.

4. Profits of a company are distributed by way of dividend which are unearned for tax purposes whereas profits of a partnership are earned income. However, the tax changes which continually take place with the Budget and subsequent Finance Acts can drastically alter how each of these is treated and should be checked at the time.

Advantages of a partnership

1. A partnership may tend to give a more personal aspect to dealings.

2. There are no heavy setting-up expenses to a partnership.

3. The activities of the partnership are not subject to restriction as with a company which is limited by the Objects

clause in its Memorandum of Association. Currently Objects clauses allow almost anything that is legal.

4. Partners may override the Partnership Act by agreement amongst themselves whereas companies have to abide by the Companies Acts.

5. All partners can take part in the management of the business and no change in the constitution can take place without the consent of all the partners. In a company the will of the majority operates but the company is normally run day to day by the board of directors.

6. Partnerships have no registration formalities.

You should by now have considered all aspects of your business and have made up your mind you would like to run your business through a company. The rest of this book explains in detail how to go about it.

CASE STUDIES

Introduction

Imagine the following three fictitious businesses have formed their own companies. The progress of these companies will be traced in the case studies throughout the succeeding chapters and this should help you understand the various facets of running a company.

Dean Chapman is a young man in his late 20s with an awareness of the growing incidence of vandalism and theft in his local town. He had seen it firsthand at the engineering factory where he worked. As an entrepreneur, however, he realised that this meant there must be an increasing demand for security both at home and in the factory and office. He therefore decided that he would quit his job and set himself up to provide solutions to vandalism and theft by security measures geared to the customer. He called his company **Chapman Security Ltd.**

Hannah Phillips had always been artistic, particularly where jewellery was concerned. Her children were now off her hands and she joined a further education class in jewellery design. It was there she met **Usha Patel**, who was clearly a talented designer concentrating on Asian designs. They became firm friends and learned techniques from one another. It became clear, as they both obtained more and more orders for their unique designs, that this could not continue as a hobby. They decided to set up shop together and with advice from an accountant formed their company **Diamond Designs Ltd**.

Harry Burgess was a successful businessman in the building industry, who had bought some property over the years which he considered to be his 'pension'. One of these properties was a mansion which he had converted into apartments. He wished to convert some of this 'pension' into cash and, finding it was difficult to sell as a whole property with tenants, he was advised to sell each apartment separately. However, this caused some complications as there were communal parts of the property, such as car parks, gardens and stairways, used by all the tenants. The solution was to form a management company to deal with these and he called it **Smiths Towers Management Co Ltd**.

ACTION POINTS AND REMINDERS

1. Who are the people directly involved in your business and what do they contribute to it?

2. Consider all the possible names you might wish to call your business.

3. Are you sure of all the products or services you intend to supply from your business?

4. Will you be a sole trader or do you need a partner?

5. Are you contemplating purchasing a 'ready made' business? If so where from?

6. Name, if applicable, your possible accountant, banker, designer, financial planner, solicitor and surveyor.

Now read the case studies again.

If, as a result of completing these answers, you are convinced that you wish to form a company proceed to Chapter 2.

(2)

Setting up and Forming Your Company

Now that you have made up your mind that you are going to run your business through a company this chapter tells you what to think about and how to plan it and includes:

- creating a separate entity
- deciding your objects
- acquiring your company
- deciding your share capital requirements
- issuing shares.

CREATING A SEPARATE ENTITY
This is fundamental.

What is a company?
In Chapter 1 you read how the concept of partnership came about and how as trade increased there was more and more of a burden on the individual partners. The property and the debts of the firm were considered to be the property and debts of the individual partners. In the nature of things partners died and, as they were no longer partners, the partnership ceased to exist.

By the mid 19th century a more permanent form of partnership evolved, known as the **joint stock company**.

This meant that a company could hold property, incur debts and sue and be sued in its own name. This was known as 'limited liability' and meant that the members (partners) were no longer personally liable for the debts of the company.

As a result of this the company exists permanently and is in effect an 'artificial' person, quite separate from the individual members of the company.

> **This is an important principle to be grasped:**
> **In your business dealings**
> **it is not *you* that is dealing**
> **but *you on behalf of your company*.**

From now on whenever the word 'company' is used please remember this important principle. All detailed legislation relating to limited companies is contained in the Companies Act 1985, with amendements in the Companies Act 1989. This is now the main statutory framework for UK company law.

DECIDING YOUR OBJECTS

Any company must define what it is and what it is for. This is done in a document known as the Memorandum of Association.

The Memorandum, in a form specified by regulations, must be submitted to the Registrar of Companies and will state, amongst other things:

- the company's name
- the place of the registered office of the company
- the objects of the company
- that the liability of the members is limited
- the amount of the share capital and its division into shares.

Let us briefly deal with each of these in turn.

Choosing the name

You can choose any name you wish, subject to a few obvious conditions. You may not choose a name if:

(a) It is already registered by someone else.

(b) It requires the approval of the Secretary of State because it is 'sensitive'. This could be so if, for example, it contains the words, International, British, European, *etc*.

(c) It contains words which other relevant bodies might object to: for example, Police, Royal, Charity, *etc*.

This list is by no means exhaustive but you can see the difficulties that may arise if your intended name is too similar to that of another company or gives the impression that it is something which it is not. Watch this carefully as that other company could object and your company be directed to change its name with the additional expense that entails.

> **Be careful to clear your intended name with the Registrar of Companies first.**

Example

Acceptable   –   Chapman Security Ltd.

Not acceptable –   Police Security Systems Ltd.

Locating the registered office

This is the 'official' address of the company where anyone can get in touch and where certain statutory information is held. The Memorandum only asks you to state whether it is in England and Wales, or in Wales, or in Scotland. Once this 'domicile', as it is known, is established the actual address can be moved within that domicile but not outside it. For example, if the domicile is England the address can be changed from Liverpool to London but not Liverpool to Glasgow.

Example

The Registered Office of the company will be situate in England.

Defining the objects

Although a company can, as a separate legal person, acquire rights and incur liabilities, its powers are slightly less extensive than a real person. A real person can do anything not prohibited by law but a company can **only do what is authorised by the objects clause in its Memorandum**.

It is not, however, necessary to go into great detail here as it is generally recognised that the main object of the business can be defined by a very general trading clause which will

THE COMPANIES ACTS 1985–1989

COMPANY LIMITED BY SHARES

MEMORANDUM
OF ASSOCIATION

SINCLAIR BROOK LIMITED

PRIVATE LIMITED COMPANY NUMBER: 2958141

INCORPORATED : 12th August 200X

ALPHA SEARCHES AND FORMATIONS LIMITED
54–58 Caledonian Road,
London N1 9RN

Fig. 1. Sample Memorandum of Association.

THE COMPANIES ACTS 1985–1989

COMPANY LIMITED BY SHARES

MEMORANDUM OF ASSOCIATION OF
SINCLAIR BROOK LIMITED

1. The name of the Company is: SINCLAIR BROOK LIMITED.

2. The registered office of the Company will be situate in England.

3. The objects for which the Company is established are:

(a) To carry on business as a general commercial company.

(b) To carry on any other business of any description whatsoever which may seem to the Company or in the opinion of the Board of Directors thereof to be advantageously carried on in connection with or ancillary to the objects of the Company or any of them and calculated directly or indirectly to render more profitable the Company's business.

(c) To purchase or by any other means acquire, sell, lease, rent, license, surrender, accept surrenders of, mortgage, charge or otherwise deal in any freehold, leasehold or other property wheresoever situate.

(d) To erect, construct, pull down, dismantle, remove or replace, repair and maintain, alter, hire, enlarge and adapt any buildings both portable and otherwise and use the same for the Company's businesses or any of them.

(e) To purchase or by any other means acquire, take over and undertake all or any part of the business, property, liabilities and assets of any person, firm or company carrying on or formed to carry on any business for which this Company is authorised to carry on or possessed of property suitable to the purposes of this Company and which is calculated to advance the interests of this Company and make more profitable the Company's business and to pay cash or to issue shares, stock, debentures or debenture stock of this Company as the consideration for such purpose of acquisition and to undertake any liabilities or obligations relating to the business or property so purchased or acquired.

(f) To buy, sell, export, import, manufacture, exchange or part exchange, let on hire, build, construct, install, erect, enlarge, improve, adapt, dismantle, remodel, repair and maintain any engine, machinery, plant and material of any description capable of being conveniently made, used or sold in any of the businesses or trades aforesaid.

Fig. 1. (continued).

(g) To enter into partnership or any arrangement of any kind with any person, persons, firm or company having for its objects similar objects to those of this Company or any of them with a view to increasing the business of the Company.

(h) To purchase, subscribe for or otherwise acquire shares, stock or other interests in any company or corporation.

(i) To act as agents or brokers for any person, firm or company and to undertake and perform sub-contracts for any person, persons, firms or companies and also to appoint such agents, sub-contractors and brokers and to act in any of the businesses of the Company through them.

(j) To apply for, register, purchase or by any means acquire and protect and prolong and renew any trade marks, patents, licences, concessions and designs which may be capable of being dealt with by the Company or likely to benefit the Company and to grant licences or privileges thereout.

(k) To sell, let, license, develop, improve or otherwise deal with the undertaking of all or any part of the property or assets of the Company, upon such terms as the Company may approve with power to accept shares, debentures or securities of, or interests in, any other company.

(l) To borrow and raise money in such manner as the Company shall think fit and in particular by the issue of debentures or debenture stock charged upon all or any of the Company's property both present and future including its uncalled capital and to re-issue any debentures at any time paid off.

(m)To draw, make, accept, endorse, discount, negotiate, execute and issue promissory notes, bills of exchange, bills of lading, warrants, debentures and other negotiable instruments.

(n) To guarantee the payment of any debentures, debenture stock, mortgages, charges, bonds, obligations, interests, dividends, securities, monies or shares or the performance of contracts or engagements of any other company or person and to give indemnities and guarantees of all kinds whenever considered desirable and to guarantee either by personal obligation or by mortgaging or charging all or any part of the undertaking property and assets both present and future and uncalled capital of the Company or by both such methods, the performance of any contract or obligation of any person, firm or company whatsoever.

(o) To invest and deal with the monies of the Company not immediately required in such shares or upon such securities and in such manner and on such conditions as may from time to time be determined.

Fig. 1. (continued).

(p) To lend and advance money and give credit to any persons, firms or companies on such terms and conditions as the Company may decide.

(q) To make advances to customers and others and allow them credit without security to enable them to purchase the goods, produce and products of the Company or use its services and for any other purpose calculated to enhance the Company's business.

(r) To promote the Company's interests by advertising its products, works or services in any manner and to take part in competitions, displays and exhibitions and offer prizes, gifts and concessions to customers or prospective customers as might seem desirable.

(s) To remunerate any person, firm or company rendering services to this Company in any manner whatsoever.

(t) To grant pensions to employees and ex-employees and Directors and ex-Directors or other Officers of the Company, their widows, children and dependants and to subscribe to benevolent and other funds for the benefit of any such persons and to subscribe to and assist any charitable association and assist in the promotion thereof.

(u) To pay all and any expenses incurred in connection with the promotion, formation and incorporation of this Company and to promote or aid in the promotion of any other companies.

(v) To distribute any property of the Company in specie among the Members of the Company.

(w) To procure the Company to be registered or recognised in any part of the world.

(x) To do all such other things as are incidental or conductive to the attainment of the above objects or any of them.

It is declared that the foregoing sub-clauses or any of them shall be construed independently of each other and none of the objects herein mentioned shall be deemed to be merely subsidiary to the objects contained in any other sub-clauses.

4. The liability of the Members is limited.

5. The Share Capital of the Company is £1,000 divided into 1,000 Ordinary Shares of £1 each, each with power to increase or to divide the shares in the capital for the time being into different classes having such rights, privileges and advantages as to voting or otherwise as the Articles of Association may from time to time prescribe.

WE, the persons whose names and addresses are subscribed are

Fig. 1. (continued).

desirous of being formed into a Company in pursuance of the Memorandum of Association and we respectively agree to take the number of shares in the capital of the Company set opposite our respective names.

Names, addresses and description of subscribers	Shares taken by each subscriber
ALPHA SECRETARIAL 54/58 Caledonian Road London N1 9RN Limited Company	ONE
ALPHA DIRECT LIMITED 54/58 Caledonian Road London N1 9RN Limited Company	ONE
Dated: 1st August 200X	

Witness to the above signatures:
ALPHAWIT LIMITED
54/58 Caledonian Road
London
N1 9RN

Fig. 1. (continued)

not inhibit the company from carrying out any of the objects it wishes.

In other words, for all intents and purposes, you will be able to do anything you wish within reason and within the law.

Example
The objects for which the Company is established are:

(a)   To carry on business as a general commercial company.

(b) To carry on any other business of any description whatsoever which may seem to the company or in the opinion of the Board of Directors thereof to be advantageously carried on in connection with or ancillary to the
objects of the company or any of them and calculated
directly or indirectly to render more profitable the
company's business.

(c) . . . to . . . (x) Clauses . . . To cover all those normal business transactions and dealings carried out by the majority of companies.

Limiting your liability

The fourth clause of a Memorandum provides that the liability of the members shall be limited. What does this actually
mean?

In simple terms it states that no member, meaning a shareholder, is liable to contribute any more than the nominal
value of his shares. Once you have paid for your shares that
is the extent of your liability. This is obviously a comforting
thought if anything goes wrong.

Example
The liability of the members is limited.

Calculating your capital

The Memorandum must state the amount of the authorised
capital, sometimes known as the nominal capital, and the
division of that capital into shares showing the value of each.
There can be different classes of shares but for this purpose
we will assume there is only one.

Example

The Share Capital of the company is £1,000 divided into 1,000 Ordinary Shares of £1 each.

ACQUIRING YOUR COMPANY

There are two ways of setting yourself up in business. You can do this by:

- starting a business on your own or in partnership
- buying an existing business.

Either of these can be put into a company and, indeed, the latter may already exist as a company.

Starting your own business

If you are setting up your business on your own you may wish to start with a brand new company. This can be done in two ways.

1. Buy a new or custom made company with your own choice of name. Various forms will have to be signed.

2. Buy a ready made company which has never traded. This is known as buying a company **off the shelf**.

Both of these methods can most easily be done through a **company formation** or **registration agent**. A telephone call to one of them will set the ball rolling but you must have your company name and address ready. Alternatively the agent will have a bank of ready made companies already named for you to choose from if you wish.

The agent will then send you the details of the company with your chosen name. He or she will probably arrange for themselves to be company secretary and for the original sub-scriber shares to be issued. There are usually two subscriber shares, but a company may exist with only one. The shares are normally put in the agent's and a colleague's name for convenience as it saves having to get your signature every time something needs to be done.

Once he or she is satisfied that the company is properly formed you will be sent:

◆ Form 10 which you will complete with names of the first directors and the intended address of the registered office (see Figure 2).
◆ Form 288c which will change the particulars of the secretary from the agent to your chosen name (see Figure 3).

What about the cost?

You will at this stage have to pay an amount between roughly £100 and £300 depending on the amount contained in the agent's package. This may be an economy package containing the basic legal requirements with a simple register of the company's history at say £110. It may be a regular package with additional copies of your Memorandum and Articles and a better register at say £140 or it may be a de luxe package with a brass name plate and your Certificate of Incorporation in a frame. It will be your choice but you should have more, rather than fewer, copies of the Memorandum and Articles as these may become useful when dealing with banks and other funders who may wish to see or retain a copy.

Once all the forms have been signed and sent to the Registrar of Companies and you have received your Certificate of Incorporation (see Figure 4) you are ready to trade.

10

Please complete in typescript, or in bold black capitals.

First directors and secretary and intended situation of registered office

Notes on completion appear on final page

2958141

Company Name in full SINCLAIR BROOK LIMITED

F 0 1 0 0 0 1 H

Proposed Registered Office 5 RIDGE PLACE

(PO Box numbers only, are not acceptable)

Post town WARE

County / Region HERTS Postcode SG51 2PY

If the memorandum is delivered by an agent for the subscriber(s) of the memorandum mark the box opposite and give the agent's name and address.

Agent's Name ALPHA SEARCHES & FORMATIONS LTD.

Address 54-58 CALEDONIAN ROAD,

Post town LONDON

County / Region Postcode N1 9RN

Number of continuation sheets attached

Please give the name, address, telephone number and, if available, a DX number and Exchange of the person Companies House should contact if there is any query.

ALPHA SEARCHES & FORMATIONS LTD.
54—58 CALEDONIAN ROAD
Tel 020 7278 7813

DX number DX exchange

Companies House receipt date barcode

When you have completed and signed the form please send it to the Registrar of Companies at:

Companies House, Crown Way, Cardiff, CF4 3UZ **DX 33050 Cardiff**
for companies registered in England and Wales
or
Companies House, 37 Castle Terrace, Edinburgh, EH1 2EB
for companies registered in Scotland **DX 235 Edinburgh**

Form revised March 1995

Fig. 2. Statement of first directors and secretary and intended situation of registered office (Form 10).

Company Secretary (see notes 1-5)

	Company name	SINCLAIR BROOK LTD.
NAME	*Style / Title	MR.
	*Honours etc	
* Voluntary details	Forename(s)	ROBERT
	Surname	BROWNING
	Previous forename(s)	
	Previous surname(s)	
Address		5 RIDGE PLACE

Usual residential address
For a corporation, give the registered or principal office address.

	Post town	WARE
	County / Region	HERTS.
	Postcode	SG 51 2PY
	Country	

I consent to act as secretary of the company named on page 1

Consent signature | R Brun | Date | 1ST AUG. 200X

Directors (see notes 1-5)

Please list directors in alphabetical order

NAME	*Style / Title	MR.
	*Honours etc	
	Forename(s)	MATHEW ALEXANDER
	Surname	BROWNING
	Previous forename(s)	
	Previous surname(s)	
Address		27 HAILEYBURY STREET

Usual residential address
For a corporation, give the registered or principal office address.

	Post town	MELBOURNE
	County / Region	HERTS
	Postcode	SG 27 8KK
	Country	

	Day	Month	Year		
Date of birth	08	07	64	Nationality	BRITISH

Business occupation	CHARTERED SURVEYOR
Other directorships	NONE

I consent to act as director of the company named on page 1

Consent signature | M.A. Browning | Date | 1ST AUG. 200X

Fig. 2. (continued).

41

Directors (continued) (see notes 1-5)

NAME	*Style / Title	MRS
* Voluntary details	Forename(s)	LEESA
	Surname	BROWNING
	Previous forename(s)	
	Previous surname(s)	

*Honours etc

Address
Usual residential address
For a corporation, give the
registered or principal office
address.

	101 HOSPITAL ROAD
	WATFORD
Post town	
County / Region	HERTS
Country	

Postcode WD1 9XY

	Day	Month	Year		
Date of birth	14	06	66	Nationality	BRITISH
Business occupation	SALES EXECUTIVE				
Other directorships	NONE				

I consent to act as director of the company named on page 1

Consent signature	L. Browning	Date	1ST AUG.200X

This section must be signed by
Either

an agent on behalf of all subscribers	Signed		Date	

Or the subscribers

(*i.e those who signed as members on the memorandum of association).*	Signed		Date	
	Signed		Date	
	Signed		Date	
	Signed		Date	
	Signed		Date	
	Signed		Date	

Fig. 2. (continued).

Notes

1. Show for an individual the full forename(s) NOT INITIALS and surname together with any previous forename(s) or surname(s).

If the director or secretary is a corporation or Scottish firm - show the corporate or firm name on the surname line.

Give previous forename(s) or surname(s) except that:

- for a married woman, the name by which she was known before marriage need not be given,

- names not used since the age of 18 or for at least 20 years need not be given.

A peer, or an individual known by a title, may state the title instead of or in addition to the forename(s) and surname and need not give the name by which that person was known before he or she adopted the title or succeeded to it.

Address:

Give the usual residential address.

In the case of a corporation or Scottish firm give the registered or principal office.

Subscribers:

The form must be signed personally either by the subscriber(s) or by a person or persons authorised to sign on behalf of the subscriber(s).

2. Directors known by another description:

- A director includes any person who occupies that position even if called by a different name, for example, governor, member of council.

3. Directors details:

- Show for each individual director the director's date of birth, business occupation and nationality.
The date of birth must be given for every individual director.

4. Other directorships:

- Give the name of every company of which the person concerned is a director or has been a director at any time in the past 5 years. You may exclude a company which either **is or at all times during the past 5 years,** when the person was a director, **was:**

- dormant,

- a parent company which wholly owned the company making the return,

- a wholly owned subsidiary of the company making the return, or

- another wholly owned subsidiary of the same parent company.

If there is insufficient space on the form for other directorships you may use a separate sheet of paper, which should include the company's number and the full name of the director.

5. Use Form 10 continuation sheets or photocopies of page 2 to provide details of joint secretaries or additional directors and include the company's number.

Fig. 2. (continued).

COMPANIES HOUSE

Please complete in typescript, or in bold black capitals.

288c

CHANGE OF PARTICULARS for director or secretary (*NOT for appointment (use Form 288a) or resignation (use Form 288b)*)

Company Number	2958141
Company Name in full	SINCLAIR BROOK LIMITED

F 2 8 8 C 0 1 A

Changes of particulars form — *Complete in all cases*

Date of change of particulars — Day `01` Month `08` Year `OX`

Name

- *Style / Title: MR.
- *Honours etc:
- Forename(s): ROBERT
- Surname: BROWNING
- † Date of Birth: Day `07` Month `02` Year `37`

Change of name (*enter new name*)
- Forename(s):
- Surname:

Change of usual residential address (*enter new address*): 27 CLOCK PARADE
- Post town: WARE
- County / Region: HERTS
- Postcode: SG51 3ZZ
- Country: ENGLAND

Other change (*please specify*):

A serving director, secretary etc must sign the form below.

Signed *R. Browning* **Date** 2nd AUG. 200X

(by a serving director / secretary / administrator / administrative receiver / receiver manager / receiver)

* Voluntary details.
† Directors only.

Please give the name, address, telephone number and, if available, a DX number and Exchange of the person Companies House should contact if there is any query.

AS ABOVE

Tel

DX number | DX exchange

Companies House receipt date barcode

When you have completed and signed the form please send it to the Registrar of Companies at:
Companies House, Crown Way, Cardiff, CF4 3UZ   **DX 33050 Cardiff**
for companies registered in England and Wales   or
Companies House, 37 Castle Terrace, Edinburgh, EH1 2EB
for companies registered in Scotland   **DX 235 Edinburgh**

Form revised March 1995

Fig. 3. Change of particulars of director or secretary (Form 288c).

CERTIFICATE OF INCORPORATION

OF A PRIVATE LIMITED COMPANY

Company No. 2958141

The Registrar of Companies for England and Wales hereby certifies that
SINCLAIR BROOK LIMITED

is this day incorporated under the Companies Act 1985 as a private

company and that the company is limited.

Given at Companies House, Cardiff, the 12th August XXXX

For the Registrar of Companies

C O M P A N I E S   H O U S E

HC007A

Fig. 4. Certificate of Incorporation.

Buying an existing business

The purchase of an existing company has many facets to be considered:

- What are you buying?
- Is it what you want?
- Do you only want the assets of the business?
- Is there any goodwill?
- How much are the shares?

Remember the company is a legal entity on its own so when you buy it you buy all its debts and liabilities as well as its assets. Now note the legal requirements of purchasing an existing company.

If you buy an existing business which is in a company you will not have to go through as much formality. The company is already in existence with an acceptable name. All you have to do from a legal viewpoint, therefore, is to transfer the shares into the names of your intended shareholders and submit to the Registrar of Companies the changes in directors, secretary and registered office.

You are now ready to commence trading with your newly acquired company.

DECIDING YOUR SHARE CAPITAL REQUIREMENTS

You will recall from earlier in the chapter that the Capital Clause forms part of your Memorandum. In it you state the amount of your **authorised capital** or **nominal capital**. This is the maximum amount of shares you can issue to your shareholders.

Example

Your authorised capital is 1,000 ordinary shares of £1 each. Two are normally issued to start with and these are transferred from the agent to yourself and your other shareholder. (It is possible, but not unusual, for a company to be formed with only one shareholder.) This leaves a further 998 shares to be issued. You may decide to issue 498 of those, split between yourself and the other shareholder so that you finish up with 400 and he holds 100. This is known as **issued** or **paid up** capital. This gives you control of the company (more fully described in Chapter 4).

	You	*Other*
Subscriber shares	1	1
Allotment	399	99
Final shareholding	400	100
Authorised capital still to be issued	500 shares	

Note that the authorised capital of a company can only be changed or increased in accordance with the Articles of the company.

The Articles of Association

The Articles of Association have not been defined yet, but:

- the Memorandum defines the powers and objectives of the company
- the Articles describe the procedure by which the powers are to be exercised or the objects of the company achieved.

This is necessary because of the company's artificial

existence and it is necessary to define the powers of the shareholders and the directors and the manner in which they can be exercised.

ISSUING SHARES

The concept of issuing shares is simple. Shares have a nominal value of, say, £1 each and when they are issued to a prospective shareholder he pays £1 for them. That is the limit of his liability towards the debts and obligations of the company.

Example

1. You buy 500 shares of £1 each for £500 and the money goes into the company's bank account as part of its assets.

2. You will not have to buy any more if you do not wish but the implications of doing so are discussed in Chapter 8 under raising money.

3. This capital will remain fixed within the company and will be repayable to you as a shareholder only when the company is closed down (when you will receive, for each of your shares, the value of the company's assets divided by the number of shares issued) or in certain circumstances, when the company may wish to buy back the shares from you.

4. You are, of course, at liberty to sell the shares to another person and this can be at any price you negotiate between you and not necessarily at the £1 you originally purchased them for.

> **Be careful how you issue your shares.**

Control

The control of the company, which is the power to decide who are the directors and what the business does, rests with the shareholders. Each share they hold gives them a vote or say in the affairs of the company and therefore the more you hold the greater the say. It follows that if you hold more than half the shares you will have more than half the say and 51 per cent of the shares in a company gives you effective control of it.

In practice the shareholders normally elect the directors and it is they who decide on the day to day running of the company. Only in exceptional circumstances will the shareholders exercise their right to overturn a decision of the directors. There are some decisions that require 75 per cent of the voting members, but these are rare and fundamental to the organisation of the company.

It is therefore important to issue your shares with these thoughts in mind. If you want complete control of your company you must have more than 75 per cent of the shares.

The issue of shares in a new company is done by means of an **allotment** of the shares to the first shareholders. A Form 88(2) showing how they have been allotted must be submitted to the Registrar of Companies (see Figure 5). This shows the total number of shares allotted, the names and addresses of the shareholders and must be signed and submitted by a

COMPANIES FORM No. 88(2)

Return of allotments of shares

Pursuant to section 88(2) of the Companies Act 1985 (the Act)

To the Registrar of Companies (**address overleaf**)
(see note 1)

88(2)

(REVISED 1988)

This form replaces forms PUC2, PUC3 and 88(2)

Company number

2958141

1. Name of company

· SINCLAIR   BROOK   LIMITED

2. This section must be completed for all allotments

Description of shares †	ORDINARY		
A Number allotted	298		
B Nominal value of each	£ 1	£	£
C Total amount (if any) paid or due and payable on each share (including premium if any)	£ 1	£	£

Date(s) on which the shares were allotted
(a) [on __15TH AUGUST OX__] §, or
(b) [from _____ to _____] §

The names and addresses of the allottees and the number of shares allotted to each should be given overleaf

3. If the allotment is wholly or partly other than for cash the following information must be given (**see notes 2 & 3**)

D Extent to which each share is to be treated as paid up.
Please use percentage

E Consideration for which the shares were allotted

NOTES
1. This form should be delivered to the Registrar of Companies within one month of the (first) date of allotment.
2. If the allotment is wholly or partly other than for cash, the company must deliver to the registrar a return containing the information at D & E. The company may deliver this information by completing D & E and the delivery of the information must be accompanied by the duly stamped contract required by section 88(2)(b) of the Act or by the duly stamped prescribed particulars required by section 88(3) (Form No 88(3)).
3. Details of bonus issues should be included only in section 2.

Presenter's name address and reference (if any) :

R. BROWNING,
27 CLOCK PARADE,
WARE, HERTS.
SG51 3ZZ.

For official Use	
	Post room

Page 1

Fig. 5. Return of allotment of shares (Form 88(2)).

4. Names and addresses of the allottees

Please do not write in this margin

Names and Addresses	Number of shares allotted		
	Ordinary	Preference	Other
MATHEW ALEXANDER BROWNING 27 HAILEYBURY STREET, MELBOURNE, HERTS. SG 27 8KK	149		
LEESA BROWNING 101 HOSPITAL ROAD WATFORD HERTS WD1 9XY	149		
Total	298		

Please complete legibly, preferably in black type, or bold block lettering

Where the space given on this form is inadequate, continuation sheets should be used and the number of sheets attached should be indicated in the box opposite:

† Insert Director, Secretary, Administrator, Administrative Receiver or Receiver (Scotland) as appropriate

Signed _R. Brown_ Designation _SECRETARY_ Date _15 AUG 0X_

Companies registered in England and Wales or Wales should deliver this form to:-

The Registrar of Companies
Companies House
Crown Way
Cardiff
CF4 3UZ

Companies registered in Scotland should deliver this form to:-

The Registrar of Companies
Companies House
37 Castle Terrace
Edinburgh
EH1 2EB

Page 2

Fig. 5. (continued).

director or the secretary within 21 days of the allotment. There is no limit to the number of shareholders except that there cannot be more than the number of shares in issue. However, joint shareholders are permitted.

The receipt of the shareholder's money is acknowledged by the preparation of a 'share certificate' (see Figure 6). This gives ownership or title to the shares which must be passed back to the company for re-issue if the shares change hands.

When shares change hands it is done by means of a stock transfer form (see Figure 7) which is lodged with the company secretary, who will then issue the certificate to the new shareholder.

Case study: Dean wants it all

Dean wanted to trade through a company because he would have to hold quite a bit of stock in his security business and was worried about the liability he might have if it did not move quickly enough. He has been in touch with a company registration agent and has decided to call his company Chapman Security Ltd. The name has been cleared by the Registrar as there is no similar name on the files. He has discussed shareholdings with his accountant and being unmarried has decided to hold most of the shares himself. He has persuaded his father to hold one share and be a director and his mother to hold the post of Secretary to the company. He will have the rest of the shares, namely 999 shares, which gives him complete control of the company and ensures that his statutory obligations have been met. He pays in his £1,000 (he is paying £1 for his father's share as well) and he's ready to go.

Certificate No.............. l

SHARE CERTIFICATE

Date........ 15ᵀᴴ AUGUST 200X   No. of Shares...... 1 ᴛᴏ 500

SINCLAIR BROOK LIMITED

(Registered in England No. 2958141)

THIS IS TO CERTIFY that the undermentioned is/are the registered holder(s) of
fully paid Ordinary Shares of £1 each in Sinclair Brook Limited
subject to the **Memorandum and Articles of Association of the Company.**

NAME(S) OF HOLDER(S)   NUMBER OF SHARES

Mathew Alexander Browning   500 (FIVE HUNDRED)

27 Haileybury Street
Melbourne
Herts.
SG 27 8KK

GIVEN under the Seal of the Company

Note: No transfer of any portion of this holding will be registered unless this certificate is deposited at the Registered Office of the Company.

THIS DOCUMENT IS VALUABLE AND SHOULD BE KEPT IN A SAFE PLACE.

Fig. 6 Share certificate

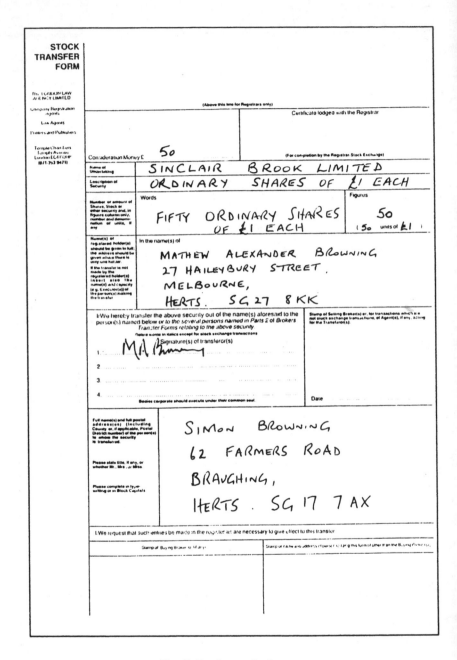

Fig. 7. Stock transfer form.

FORM OF CERTIFICATE REQUIRED WHERE TRANSFER IS EXEMPT FROM STAMP DUTY

Instruments executed on or after 1st May 1987 effecting any transactions within the following categories are exempt from stamp duty:—

A. The vesting of property subject to a trust in the trustees of the trust on the appointment of a new trustee, or in the continuing trustees on the retirement of a trustee.

B. The conveyance or transfer of property the subject of a specific devise or legacy to the beneficiary named in the will (or his nominee). Transfers in satisfaction of a general legacy of money should not be included in this category (see category D below).

C. The conveyance or transfer of property which forms part of an intestate's estate to the person entitled on intestacy (or his nominee). Transfers in satisfaction of the transferees entitlement to cash in the estate of an intestate, where the total value of the residuary estate exceeds that sum, should not be included in this category (see category D below).

D. The appropriation of property within section 84(4) of the Finance Act 1985 (death: appropriation in satisfaction of a general legacy of money) or section 84(5) or (7) of that Act (death: appropriation in satisfaction of any interest of surviving spouse and in Scotland also of any interest of issue).

E. The conveyance or transfer of property which forms part of the residuary estate of a testator to a beneficiary (or his nominee) entitled solely by virtue of his entitlement under the will.

F. The conveyance or transfer of property out of a settlement in or towards satisfaction of a beneficiary's interest, not being an interest acquired for money or money's worth, being a conveyance or transfer constituting a distribution of property in accordance with the provisions of the settlement.

G. The conveyance or transfer of property on and in consideration only of marriage to a party to the marriage (or his nominee) or to trustees to be held on the terms of a settlement made in consideration only of the marriage. A transfer to a spouse after the date of marriage is not within this category, unless made pursuant to an ante-nuptial contract.

H. The conveyance or transfer of property within section 83(1) of the Finance Act 1985 (transfers in connection with divorce etc.).

I. The conveyance or transfer by the liquidator of property which formed part of the assets of the company in liquidation to a shareholder of that company (or his nominee) in or towards satisfaction of the shareholder's rights on a winding-up.

J. The grant in fee simple of an easement in or over land for no consideration in money or money's worth.

K. The grant of a servitude for no consideration in money or money's worth.

L. The conveyance or transfer of property operating as a voluntary disposition inter vivos for no consideration in money or money's worth nor any consideration referred to in section 57 of the Stamp Act 1891 (conveyance in consideration of a debt etc.).

M. The conveyance or transfer of property by an instrument within section 84(1) of the Finance Act 1985 (death: varying disposition).

(1) Delete as appropriate

(2) Insert "(A)", "(B)" or appropriate category

(3) Delete second sentence if the certificate is given by the transferor or his solicitor

(1) I/We hereby certify that the transaction in respect of which this transfer is made is one which falls within the category(2) .... above. (I)/We confirm that (I)/We have been duly authorised by the transferor to sign certificate and that the facts of the transaction are within (I)my/our knowledge (3)

Signature(s) ....

Description ("Transferor", "Solicitor", etc.) ....

Date .... 19 ......

NOTES

(1) If the above certificate has been completed, this transfer does not need to be submitted to the Controller of Stamps but should be sent directly to the Company or its Registrars.

(2) If the above certificate is not completed, this transfer must be submitted to the Controller of Stamps and duly stamped. (See below).

FORM OF CERTIFICATE REQUIRED WHERE TRANSFER IS NOT EXEMPT BUT IS NOT LIABLE TO
AD VALOREM STAMP DUTY

Instruments of transfer, other than those in respect of which the above certificate has been completed, are liable to a fixed duty of 50p when the transaction falls within one of the following categories:—

(a) Transfer by way of security for a loan or re-transfer to the original transferor on repayment of a loan.

(b) Transfer, not on sale and not arising under any contract of sale and where no beneficial interest in the property passes: (i) to a person who a mere nominee of, and is nominated only by, the transferor; (ii) from a mere nominee who has at all times held the property on behalf of transferee; (iii) from one nominee to another nominee of the same beneficial owner where the first nominee has at all times held the property on behalf of that beneficial owner. (Note—This category does not include a transfer made in any of the following circumstances: (i) by a holder of stock, etc., following the grant of an option to purchase the stock, to the person entitled to the option or his nominee; (ii) to a nominee in contemplation of a contract for the sale of the stock, etc., then about to be entered into; (iii) from the nominee of a vendor, who has instructed the nominee orally or by some unstamped writing to hold stock, etc., in trust for a purchaser, to such purchaser.)

(1) Delete as appropriate.

(2) Insert "(a)", "(b)".

(3) Here set out concisely the facts explaining the transaction. Adjudication may be required.

(1) I/We hereby certify that the transaction in respect of which this transfer is made is one which falls within the category(2) .... above. (I)/I/we confirm that (I)I/We have been duly authorised by the transferor to sign this certificate and the facts of the transaction are within (I)my/our knowledge.

(3) ....
....
....
....

Signature(s) ....

Description ("Transferor", "Solicitor", etc.) ....

....
....

Date .... 19 ......

Fig. 7. (continued).

Case study: Hannah and Usha share it

Hannah and Usha felt they had not known each other long enough to form an ordinary partnership with the prospect of being responsible for each other's debts. On advice they decided to form a company, having half the shares each and taking out money, when available, and sharing it equally. The company was set up with £2,000 of ordinary shares of £1 each and they each put in £1,000 to purchase their half of the share capital. Hannah has agreed to be company secretary as well as a director.

Case study: Harry learns how to spread the load

Harry has always been his own master and controlled the finances of his own enterprises. But he had to come to terms with the concept of forming a company in which each of the buyers of his apartments had one share each in the company. Like all property transactions the sales took some time and he had to hold some of the shares himself until the sales actually took place. There were eleven apartments and so the company was formed with an authorised capital of £100 but only eleven shares were issued. As the sale of each apartment was completed part of the deal was that the owners purchased one share and became part of the management committee whose responsibility was to manage the communal areas of the whole property. These were the outside painting and decoration of the building and perhaps more importantly the roof. It also included the hallways, the stairs, the gardens and the parking area. A form of annual subscription would be devised by the committee to cover all these costs. There would therefore be eleven directors and one of them would become Secretary when the committee agreed.

ACTION POINTS AND REMINDERS

1. List three possible names you could choose for your company.

2. Decide who you will ask to be shareholders.

3. Consider who you would choose as co-directors.

4. Decide who you would like to be company secretary bearing in mind the legal obligations of that office. You may like to do it yourself.

5. Decide how much capital the company will need.

6. Have you decided how many shares do you intend to hold yourself?

7. Where do you intend your registered office to be? (It can be your home address, your business premises, your accountant's address (with his/her permission) or any other address which you feel would be convenient.)

8. You must now find a company agent who can help you form your company.

3

Dealing with the Formalities

Like many things in life there is a certain amount of bureaucracy to be dealt with in starting a company. This chapter looks at some of the procedures to be gone through in order to get your company up and running. They include:

- understanding the Articles of Association
- appointing your directors and the company secretary
- getting a registered office
- displaying your certificate of incorporation
- holding meetings and passing resolutions
- dealing with Companies House.

UNDERSTANDING THE COMPANY'S ARTICLES OF ASSOCIATION

Mention has been made in the previous chapters of the company's **Articles of Association**. It would be as well at this point to explain what these are. The articles are the detailed rules that determine the internal management of the company.

They will normally show amongst other things:

- which clauses of the Companies Act will not apply to the company

- details of how shares are allotted, issued and repurchased
- how share certificates are issued
- how shares are transferred and how the price will be arrived at
- what general meetings are required and for what purpose
- how resolutions and decisions at meetings are to be effected
- the rules governing directors and the secretary
- the limits of the borrowing powers of directors
- the rules for disqualifying directors from holding office
- the extent of indemnity for officials in executing their duties on behalf of the company.

If you do not decide on these for yourself then the standard rules set out in the Companies Act will apply.

APPOINTING YOUR DIRECTORS AND SECRETARY

The directors

The law has given your company a personality but it is really fictitious. It cannot do anything on its own. It is, therefore, essential that it authorises someone to conduct its business for it. Those people authorised are called **directors**.

Officially directors are appointed to manage the affairs of a company in accordance with its Articles of Association and the law generally. In addition to this a director has responsibilities and these are outlined in Chapter 5.

Sometimes directors are appointed in the Articles of Association but these appointments are actually invalid.

Note: A director is not officially appointed until a Form

**10 is submitted to the Registrar of Companies showing
details of name, address, date of birth, nationality, occupation and details of any other directorships held (see
Figure 2).**

Most modern forms of Articles of Association allow any person to be a director. That is, they do not preclude anyone who
is barred from being a director by the regulations set out in
Table A in the Companies (Tables A to F) Regulations 1985.
For example persons over 70 years of age are precluded from
being appointed under the regulations in Table A.

These regulations are put in place by the Companies Act to
apply if there is no clause in the company's own articles to
overrule them.

Directors will have an equal say in the running of the affairs
of the company irrespective of the number of shares they
may hold, if they hold any at all. It is not compulsory. Also
a director may contract with a supplier of goods or services
on behalf of the company or may enter into agreements on
behalf of the company. It is, therefore, important to choose
fellow directors wisely. They could cost the company a great
deal of money.

Case study: Dean works from home

Dean has decided that his premises, which are mainly for
holding his stock, are not suitable as an office. He therefore
agreed with his parents to use their home as his office and registered his home address as the official Registered Office of
the company. He completed Form 10 with himself as one
director, his father as the other and his mother as company

THE COMPANIES ACTS 1985–1989
COMPANY LIMITED BY SHARES

ARTICLES OF ASSOCIATION OF
SINCLAIR BROOK LIMITED

PRELIMINARY

1. The Company is a Private Company within the meaning of Section 1(3) of the Companies Act 1985. Accordingly the Company shall not offer to the public (whether for cash or otherwise) any shares in or debentures of the Company or allot or agree to allot (whether for cash or otherwise) any shares in or debentures of the Company with a view to all or any of the shares or debentures being offered for sale to the public. Subject as hereinafter provided the Regulations set out in Table "A" in the Companies (Tables A to F) Regulations 1985 shall apply to this Company.

2. The following Articles of Table "A" shall not apply to this Company, videlicet:- 24, 37, 40, 46, 50, 53, 73, 74, 75, 81, 94 and the last sentence of Article 79.

SHARE CAPITAL

3. The Directors of the Company shall within a period of five years from the date of incorporation of the Company be entitled to exercise the Company's power to allot, grant options over or otherwise dispose of the entire amount of the original share capital of the Company. The Members of the Company shall have power from time to time by Ordinary Resolution to renew or revoke the Directors' exercise of the Company's power to allot, grant options over or otherwise dispose of any shares in the capital of the Company.

4.(a) Sections 89(1), 90(1) to (5) and Section 90(6) of the Companies Act 1985 shall not apply in relation to the issue of any equity securities by the Company but in substitution therefor the provisions of sub-paragraph (b) of this Article shall apply,

   (b) Save as otherwise directed by the Company in General Meeting, any new shares from time to time to be created shall before they are issued be offered to the Members in proportion as nearly as possible to the numbers of shares held by them. Any such offer shall be made by notice specifying the number of shares offered and limiting a time within which the offer, if not accepted, will be deemed to be declined and after the expiration of such time any shares not accepted and any shares which, by reason of the ratio which the shares to be issued bear to the shares held by persons entitled to an offer thereof, cannot, in the opinion of the Directors, conveniently be offered under this Article, shall be at the disposal of the Directors who may allot, grant options over, or otherwise dispose of the same

Fig. 8. Sample Articles of Association.

15. In the case of any equality of votes at any Director's Meeting, the Chairman of the Meeting shall not have a second or casting vote and Article 88 of Table A shall be modified accordingly.

16. Subject to the provisions of Section 317 of the Companies Act 1985, a Director may contract with the Company and participate in the profits of any contracts or arrangements as if he were not a Director. A Director shall also be capable of voting in respect of such contracts or arrangements, where he has previously disclosed his interest to the Company, or in respect of his appointment to any office or place of profit under the Company, or in respect of the terms there of and may be counted in the quorum at any Meeting at which any such matter is considered.

    SECRETARY

17. The first Secretary of the Company shall be the person or persons named as Secretary in the Statement delivered under Section 10(2) of the Companies Act 1985 and deemed to be appointed accordingly.

    BORROWING POWERS OF THE DIRECTORS

18. The Directors of the Company may exercise all the powers of the Company to borrow money whether in excess of the nominal amount of the share capital of the Company for the time being issued or not and to mortgage or charge its undertaking, property or uncalled capital, or any part thereof, and, subject to Section 80 of the Companies Act 1985, to issue debentures, debenture stock and other securities whether outright or as security for any debt, liability or obligation of the Company or of any third party.

    ALTERNATE DIRECTORS

19. Any Director may in writing appoint any person to be his alternate to act in his place at any meeting of the Directors at which he is unable to be present. Every such alternate shall be entitled to notice of meetings of the Directors and to attend and vote thereat as a Director when the person appointing him is not personally present and where he is a Director to have a separate vote on behalf of the Director he is representing in addition to his own vote. A Director may at any time in writing revoke the appointment of an alternate appointed by him. Every such alternate shall be an officer of the Company and shall not be deemed to be the agent of the Director appointing him. The remuneration of such an alternate shall be payable out of the remuneration payable to the Director appointing him and the proportion thereof shall be agreed between them. An alternate need not hold any share qualification.

    THE SEAL

20. Article 101 of Table A shall be read and construed as if the words "The Seal" were followed by the words "if any".

Fig. 8. (continued).

INDEMNITY

21. Subject to Section 310 of the Companies Act 1985 and in addition to such indemnity as is contained in Clause 118 of Table A, every Director, Officer or Official of the Company shall be indemnified out of the funds of the Company against all costs, charges, losses, expenses and liabilities incurred by him in the execution and discharge of his duties or in relation thereto.

DISQUALIFICATION OF DIRECTORS

22. The office of a Director shall be vacated:
    (1) If by notice in writing to the Company he resigns the office of Director.
    (2) If he ceases to be a Director by virtue of Section 291 of the Companies Act 1985.
    (3) If he becomes bankrupt or insolvent or enters into any arrangements with his creditors.
    (4) If he becomes of unsound mind.
    (5) If he is prohibited from being a Director by an order made under the Company Directors Disqualification Act 1986.
    (6) If he is removed from office by a Resolution duly passed under Section 303 of the Companies Act 1985.

Names, addresses and description of subscribers.

ALPHA SECRETARIAL LIMITED
54/58 Caledonian Road
London
N1 9RN
Limited Company

ALPHA DIRECT LIMITED
54/58 Caledonian Road
London
N1 9RN
Limited Company

Dated: 1st August 200X

Witness to the above signatures:
ALPHAWIT LIMITED
54/58 Caledonian Road
London N1 9RN

Fig. 8. (continued).

secretary and sent these in to the Registrar via his company formation agent.

The company secretary

The secretary of a company is the legal guardian of the company. The company secretary sees that the rules and procedures of the company are being adhered to and records all the formal proceedings. A company secretary does not have to be a lawyer but should be someone who appreciates that the law is important and carries out formalities diligently.

The responsibilities of the company secretary include:

1. Recording minutes of meetings.

2. Maintaining a register of shareholders.

3. Dealing with the formalities of any share dealings.

The company secretary is responsible to the directors. Firms of accountants or solicitors may offer to prepare the formal documents required with the secretary just signing them.

GETTING A REGISTERED OFFICE

Every company must have an official address. This is called the **registered office**.

The purpose of a registered office is so that there is an address to which notices and other communications can be sent. The Registrar is notified of the address of the first registered office when Form 10 is completed (see Figure 2) and submitted on the formation of the company. Any change in the address must be notified to the Registrar within 14 days of the change.

Remember that the 'domicile' (eg England or Scotland) must remain the same (see page 31).

Your registered office can be any address. It may be your business address or your home address or it may be the address of your accountant or solicitor. Their permission should, of course, be obtained first.

Any official document, like a writ, can be served on the company at its official registered office and will be deemed to have been delivered to the company. You cannot turn round and make the excuse that it was delivered to your accountant!

DISPLAYING YOUR CERTIFICATE OF INCORPORATION

When your Memorandum and Articles have been registered with the Registrar of Companies he will issue a signed certificate, known as the Certificate of Incorporation (see Figure 4) which is the conclusive evidence that your company is actually in existence in accordance with the Companies Act. You may now commence business.

Your Certificate of Incorporation must be displayed in a prominent position at your principal place of business. There are rules about companies displaying certain information for the benefit of the public at large. This is proof to them that the company is bona fide and that they are trading with a legitimate business.

Case study: Hannah and Usha set up shop

Hannah and Usha have rented a small workshop at the back of a retail store in the High Street. This is ideal for making their jewellery as well as getting their supplies from other traders. They seek permission from their landlord to use the workshop as their official business address and he agrees. On receipt of their Certificate of Incorporation they proudly put it up on the door of the workshop to show to anyone who comes in that Diamond Designs Ltd is officially in business.

HOLDING MEETINGS AND PASSING RESOLUTIONS

Holding meetings

You are now aware that the ultimate responsibility for the conduct of any company lies with the shareholders, even though the directors make most of the management decisions.

It is therefore necessary for a company to give its shareholders a platform from which to exercise their responsibility. This is usually in the form of a meeting and may be:

◆ the company's annual general meeting
◆ an extraordinary general meeting
◆ any general meeting called for a specific purpose.

There are strict rules governing meetings and these are normally contained in the Articles of Association. These will cover:

◆ how the Chairman of the meeting will be appointed
◆ how many members (shareholders) must be present for the meeting to transact any business (this is known as a **quorum**)
◆ how much notice must be given to each member that such a meeting is going to take place.

The Chairman of a meeting will normally be the chairman of the company or the principal shareholder. However, it is customary that the Articles will allow for any member present at the meeting to be elected chairman.

In general there must be two people present to constitute a meeting unless the Articles provide for a different number. Directors may call general meetings, including the Annual General Meeting, by giving required notice. In addition members may, in accordance with the Companies Act 1985, require the directors to convene an extraordinary general meeting.

These formal meetings are held where important matters relating to the running of the company are discussed and, if necessary, voted upon.

The annual general meeting (AGM) is normally used as a reporting meeting to give the shareholders a résumé of the year's events and results and to present the accounts for the preceding financial year.

An extraordinary meeting is usually called where there is a dispute to be settled, but in very small companies these are more likely to be personality clashes and will probably not be resolved by a formal meeting.

Passing resolutions

Decisions are taken at meetings by passing resolutions.

What is a resolution?
It is an agreement by those entitled to vote at a meeting on

any lawful matter brought before it. A proposed resolution is called a **motion**. When a motion is passed the company is bound by it until circumstances alter or another motion is passed superceding it. If the necessary majority of votes is not obtained the motion fails.

There are a number of differing types of resolution.

Directors' resolutions

These are used at directors' board meetings and are used for normal management business. They are not normally required to be filed with the Registrar of Companies, but a record should be kept so that the content may be referred to at a later date in the event of a difference of opinion.

Ordinary resolutions

These are passed by a simple majority of the votes cast and are used for matters not requiring another type of resolution. Unless otherwise stated all resolutions are ordinary resolutions. A **proxy** (someone to vote on your behalf) may be allowed in some circumstances.

Private companies may resolve problems by written resolution without a meeting being held and without formal notice provided it is a matter which could be passed by the company in general meeting. However, the resolution can only be passed by the unanimous agreement of all those members who would be entitled to attend and vote at such a meeting. The date of this resolution would be the date the last person signed.

These resolutions must also be sent to the auditors.

Case study: Harry has a meeting

Harry has formed his company with the official address registered at his principal place of business together with his other companies. It is not his intention that this company should make a profit but rather that it should be used for the benefit of all the tenants. As Harry only has two tenants installed as owners so far he transfers a share to each of them and calls the first meeting. The tenants elect him as chairman and he proposes a resolution that there will be no further meetings until all the apartments have been sold. This is carried as he has nine of the shares but it is with the agreement of the other two as well. It is in everyone's interest to set this company up properly and one of the apartment holders agrees to be company secretary temporarily until a full meeting can be held to formally elect directors and a secretary on a more permanent basis.

Extraordinary resolutions

These require a 75 per cent majority and are used for specific matters like winding up the company or changing the rights of shareholders. Members are entitled to 21 days' notice of such a resolution unless at least 95 per cent of the shareholders agree to a shorter notice. The Articles may allow proxies.

Special resolutions

These also require a 75 per cent majority and normally 21 days' notice to shareholders and are used for changes like an alteration to the Memorandum and Articles or a change of name.

Elective resolutions

These are a relatively new type of resolution brought in by the Companies Act 1989. They must be used in private companies only and must have unanimous support of the members. They are used for five specific purposes:

1. To alter the duration of the authority of directors to allot securities.

2. To dispense with the holding of annual general meetings.

3. To dispense with the laying of accounts and reports before the members in general meeting.

4. To reduce the majority required to authorise short notice of a meeting and notice of a resolution from 95 per cent but not lower than 90 per cent.

5. To dispense with the annual appointment of auditors.

Very few private company resolutions have to be sent to the Registrar of Companies for filing. Those which do are specified by the Companies Acts and include all special, extraordinary and elective resolutions and must be filed within 15 days of them being passed.

Example of elective resolution

It was resolved that in accordance with the provisions of Section 366A of the Companies Act 1985 the company hereby dispenses with the holding of the Annual General Meeting for 200X and subsequent years.

DEALING WITH COMPANIES HOUSE

It will be apparent by now that the Registrar of Companies requires private companies to keep him/her informed on certain matters. Companies are to that extent public property and the files are available for public inspection.

It is the duty of the directors and the job of the company secretary to submit various forms and resolutions to Companies House within prescribed time limits. The penalty for not doing so is normally a hefty fine. In extreme circumstances the company will be struck off the register.

It is in your interest to fulfil your obligations as people who deal with you can easily lose confidence in you as a business person if you do not.

Statutory information to be sent to the Registrar includes

- changes of the registered office
- changes of directors and secretary or their particulars
- annual returns
- copies of extraordinary, elective and special resolutions
- details of any mortgages or charges on the company property
- resolutions to change the Memorandum and Articles
- notification that the company has gone into liquidation or receivership.

ACTION POINTS AND REMINDERS

1. Ask your company formation agent for a sight of the Articles of Association before he completes the registration.

2   Decide who your directors will be.

3. Decide how many shares will you issue to each.

4. Ensure that your company secretary knows what obligations the post carries.

5. Do you have the address of your registered office organised?

6. Where will you display your certificate of incorporation?

7. Where will you hold official company meetings?

8. Will you insist on being chairman yourself?

9. You do realise that you are responsible for statutory information being sent to the Registrar.

$$\boxed{4}$$

Being a Shareholder

Now that your company is set up there are various aspects of being a shareholder to consider. This chapter deals with the more important of those aspects and in particular:

- paying yourself
- using your voting power
- exercising your rights
- paying dividends
- limiting your liability.

PAYING YOURSELF

One of the first things that anyone starting a company wants to know is how do they get payment out of the business for their own labours.

If you are a sole trader or are in partnership you can in theory just take the money when you want to. This is commonly known as **drawings** as you are drawing out money on account of profits that you hope will be made. The tax on these 'earnings' is paid later when the profit figures are known.

In a company things are different. As the company is a separate entity it has to pay you either:

- as an employee by means of a wage, a salary or by commission, or

◆   as a shareholder by way of dividend.

Let us consider the implications of each of these in turn.

Payment by wage, salary or commission

A company is required to pay all employees, and that includes directors and the company secretary, assuming they are paid at all, under the PAYE system so that tax is deducted directly at the time of payment. Paying your taxes is discussed further in Chapter 10 but suffice to say if you intend to pay yourself from your company you will have to do it in accordance with the rules that apply to all employees.

You will therefore have to decide how much money your company can afford to pay you and treat that as a wage or salary on a regular basis. Subsequently, you may find that you are taking too much which either starves the company of cash resources needed for the business or means that the company is just not making enough profit. You will then have to waive your salary for a while till business picks up. What you must not do, in these circumstances, is just draw money out as you would as a sole trader or partnership. The reason for this is simple. The company is a separate entity so if you just draw money out the company is, in effect, lending you money.

NOTE WELL
**Companies are not allowed by law to lend money
to directors.**

---

and

EQUALLY

**It is unlawful for companies to pay directors any
remuneration 'free of tax'.**

This may seem harsh because there is a tendency to think of
the money in your company as your own but it is not. It
belongs to the company. And the company, like people, has
to pay its tax. It is known as corporation tax and the rate is
fixed each year by the Government in the Budget proposals.
For small companies it is normally a similar rate to the standard rate of income tax. From July 1999 companies are
required to assess their own profits on a similar system to the
rules applying to income tax.

Case study: Hannah and Usha decide on equal salaries

Hannah and Usha have decided to pay themselves a small
salary whilst the business builds up. They contact the Inland
Revenue to ask what they should do and receive in return a
package of information described as a *New Employers
Starter Pack*. This contains all the forms and instructions for
taxing wages and salaries under the PAYE system and
accounting for their national insurance contributions. As they
only want to pay themselves as directors and have no other
employees they read the information carefully to see what is
required. They realise their tax has to be paid each month.

Payment by dividend

The profits of a company can be distributed to the shareholders by way of dividend. This means the company
decides to pay out so much per share and all shareholders

will participate. This may prove difficult if all you are trying to do is pay yourself.

Example

Your company pays a dividend to its shareholders on 31st December. There are 1000 shares in issue and you and your directors declare a dividend of £2 per share. The company will pay corporation tax on the profits and your shareholders will receive, in respect of each share they hold, £2. The cost to the company is greater by the amount of the tax paid but shareholders will get a tax credit for each share in respect of the corporation tax paid, meaning that the tax is already paid on this income when they receive it, and no more tax at the basic rate is payable by them. They could, however, pay income tax at a higher rate if their overall income is high enough.

There is more information on corporation tax in Chapter 10.

Fringe benefits

There is a further way of paying yourself in a company which should be mentioned. **Fringe benefits** are where the company pays money on your behalf for certain services. The most common fringe benefit is the provision of a company car. The amount upon which tax is payable is a percentage of the list price of the car inclusive of accessories, delivery charges and VAT, but the percentage is reduced depending on the age of the car and the business miles covered. Also note that companies have to pay national insurance on the taxable value of an employee's company car.

Other benefits you might enjoy include meals in a canteen provided all employees are entitled to them or the cost of an insurance premium which would pay you if you were unable to work.

Additionally benefits are treated just as if you had earned the money and you are taxed at the rate applicable to your salary plus your benefits less anything you contribute to them. However, this applies only if that figure is £8,500 or more or if you are a director.

Minimising your tax bill

The way you pay yourself is crucial when you are trying to minimise your tax bill. Ideally you will pay yourself the amount at which the tax rate is equal or lower than the tax rate on the company's profits. Anything above that will attract the higher rate of income tax and that is higher than the small companies corporation tax rate.

The decision of what to pay yourself is complicated and you would do well to take advice from your accountant before you start. However, in the end you will pay yourself what you need for your standard of living or what the company can afford. And you will personally have to bear the tax on that figure.

USING YOUR VOTING POWER

You saw in Chapter 3 that votes are taken, where necessary, at formal meetings of the company and each shareholder has a vote for each share owned. If, therefore, you hold a majority of the shares you will get a majority of the votes and this will enable you to carry out any changes or policy decisions you wish to.

If, however, you only hold 40 per cent of the shares there are potentially 60 per cent against you. It is rare in small companies to have such disagreements and probable that, if it were the case, the problem is fundamental and another course of action will be required to resolve it.

In most small companies the only formal decisions to take are at the annual general meeting and those normally involve:

♦ receiving the report of the directors
♦ adoption of the accounts for the previous financial year
♦ re-election of certain directors if the articles require them to stand down
♦ election or re-election of the auditor (if the company has one).

You would be well advised to think carefully how your shares are distributed amongst the shareholders, as most decisions are put to a normal majority vote.

Case study: Harry sets the charges

Harry's company was beginning to incur expense in maintaining gardens at the flats and he thought he would charge the tenants on a pro rata basis for their shares of the expense. Although they had agreed at the first meeting not to hold another one before the flats were sold he uses his prerogative to summon a meeting to put his resolution that a charge should be made. Although the other shareholders object, albeit with tongue in cheek as they realise the jobs must be done, Harry uses the power of his nine shares to push the resolution through. All the tenants from now on will pay fixed maintenance charges.

EXERCISING YOUR RIGHTS

You will not normally be required to exercise most of your rights as a shareholder in a small company. These are put in place by the various Companies Acts and by the provisions of the Memorandum and Articles to deal with intractable problems you may encounter as a shareholder. Should you be involved in a difficult area of company law you must seek advice from a lawyer or accountant as there are precedents (*ie* similar cases that have happened before) for a number of things which can occur.

Knowing what your rights are

There are certain rights that you will be involved in on a regular basis. As a shareholder you are entitled to:

- receive proper notice of any meeting of the company together with copies of any proposed resolutions so that you can attend and vote on them
- receive the financial accounts of the company for the preceding year
- transfer your shares to someone else by agreeing the price with the directors; it is often usual, according to the Articles, for these shares to be offered to the remaining shareholders in the same proportion that they hold their existing shares so that their voting rights do not alter
- call an extraordinary general meeting of the company
- be involved in any reconstruction of the way the company is financed, the sale of the company or its amalgamation with another company
- concur in the modification or variation of any rights, privileges or liabilities attached to the shares.

It is to be hoped that your company will be well run and any difficulties cleared before you need to exercise your rights. But there must be provision for the unexpected or unforeseen.

PAYING DIVIDENDS

Earlier in this chapter we saw how shareholders could be paid by dividend and the consequent tax implications. Directors recommend dividends. This is done by taking into account the financial position of the company at that time.

Types of dividend

There are two types of dividend:

- interim
- final.

Interim dividends can be declared by the directors at any time and a meeting of shareholders is not required to sanction this. The **final dividend** is agreed by the shareholders at a general meeting when they will also formally agree any interim dividend previously paid. In the absence of any provision to the contrary in the Articles dividends must always be paid in cash. They must also be paid out of profits.

An equal amount is paid for each share owned but in some companies there can be different classes of shares.

Example
A company is set up with two classes of shares:

1. preference shares

2. ordinary shares.

Preference shares are entitled to a dividend before ordinary shares are. It is usually at a fixed rate and is payable whether the company is doing well or not. Holders of preference shares have put money into the company as a fairly safe investment with a small return of interest. Ordinary shares are much more linked to the fortunes of the company and dividends can vary a lot. Sometimes no dividends are paid at all.

It is probably fair to say that in the majority of small companies payment of dividends is rare as profits are invariably taken as director's salary or other fringe benefits.

LIMITING YOUR LIABILITY

Small companies are in the main set up for one reason, and one reason alone, and that is to limit the financial liability of the shareholders to the amount of the nominal value of the shares they have purchased.

With no limited liability all of a person's assets, including his house, are available to his creditors (the people he owes money to). A limited company, which is a separate legal entity from its individual shareholders and directors, has its own assets and liabilities. But these are nothing to do with the directors or the shareholders personally and hence their liability for the company's financial debts and responsibilities is limited. Unless, of course, the directors have been trading fraudulently.

That all seems fine. But beware.

Other businesses have become aware that unscrupulous businessmen have taken advantage of this limited liability and run off with the company money or assets. Also when you are embarking on a new business venture you have to build up your credibility before you are fully trusted. Therefore you may be asked for personal guarantees against your business debts. Note that:

- banks, in particular, will ask for guarantees for an overdraft facility or a loan
- this can also apply to leasing agreements
- landlords may also consider this in respect of rent
- even normal suppliers may insist on it for normal credit arrangements.

Once any of them do this your limited liability is severely impaired. Do not think that limited liability removes all your business worries. It can sometimes make them more of a headache.

Dean wants an overdraft

Dean now has to stock up from his suppliers and they are being very helpful. After all Dean will be selling their products to his customers. However, there is a lead time between his sale to his customers and them paying. So Dean went to see his bank manager. He had prepared himself for this meeting by forecasting his expected sales and expenses and the amounts he would pay for stock. The bank manager agreed to let him have a small overdraft facility to cover this money shortfall but only on two conditions. Firstly that he prepared a cash flow chart to see where his predictions would produce the greatest shortfall and secondly that he gave a personal guarantee to repay the bank from his own resources if the company could not pay. So much for his limited liability.

ACTION POINTS AND REMINDERS

1. Decide how much to pay yourself but don't overdo it.

2. How will you pay your tax? It is due each month.

3. See your accountant about paying dividends and make sure it is necessary.

4. If you are having a company owned car you must keep adequate and accurate records of the expense.

5. Make sure you own the majority of the shares.

6. You may have to give someone dealing with your company a personal guarantee so be prepared.

⑤

Being a Director

Your company is now set up. Your registered office is fixed, your directors and secretary are in place, your shareholders have paid in their money and the rest of the formalities are complete.

You must now carefully check through your responsibilities as a director. This chapter looks at those responsibilities in more depth and includes:

- ◆ fulfilling your responsibilities
- ◆ wrongful trading
- ◆ completing your annual return
- ◆ filing your accounts
- ◆ notifying changes in your company set up.

FULFILLING YOUR RESPONSIBILITIES

Directors, as guardians of their companies, are appointed to manage the affairs of a company. This includes keeping the affairs of the company within the law and there are some legal requirements of the Companies Act which must be carried out.

Every director has a personal responsibility to see that certain documents are delivered to the Registrar of Companies. They include:

- the company's annual accounts
- the Annual Return
- notification of any change of directors or their particulars
- notification of any change of secretary or their particulars
- notification of a change of registered office
- notification of any mortgages or charges levied on the company
- notification of any changes in the Memorandum or Articles of Association
- notification of the company going into liquidation or receivership.

If you fail to send in your accounts on time a rising scale of fines is imposed, which can amount to £1,000 in a private company, if the documents are over twelve months late. It only applies to accounts and is known as a late filing penalty. It is payable by the company. Note that there can also be fines levied on a director personally for not delivering accounts, but this would only be as a result of his prosecution for the offence and would be set by the court.

Failure to submit the other documents can also result in fines on the director personally.

> *How do you avoid fines and penalties?*
> *Simple.*
>
> **Ensure that your accounts, your annual return and any other documents are submitted well on time.**

Documents have to be sent to:

The Registrar of Companies
Crown Way
Cardiff CF4 3UZ

for companies in England and Wales. There are other offices if you prefer to deliver them by hand and these are in London, Manchester, Birmingham and Leeds.

For companies in Scotland documents should be sent to:

The Registrar of Companies
Companies House
37 Castle Terrace
Edinburgh EH1 2EB

There is also an office in Glasgow for hand deliveries.

A number of companies delegate the responsibilities for sending in documents to their accountants or financial advisers as they usually prepare the accounts and are in possession of the other relevant information. Again beware. It is your job as a director to make sure the job is being done.

> **It is not your accountants or financial advisers who get prosecuted or penalised.**
> **It is YOU.**

Finally, all this statutory information is needed to make it available for public inspection. This enables other individuals or businesses to form a view of a company with which they may wish to deal. It is also part of the protection which is necessary if companies are going to have the benefit of limited liability.

Case study: Dean delegates

Dean has noted the long list of his legal responsibilities and decided that he will delegate these to his accountant. Although his mother is the company secretary she is not fully familiar with company law and is also happy to see someone who is dealing with the company formalities. The accountant explains that the necessary forms will be completed when the accounts are prepared and, although there will be a small charge for the extra work involved, he will see that all the forms are dealt with on time. All Dean has to do is check that the forms do come with the accounts when they are sent to him.

WRONGFUL TRADING

As a director you ought to know if your company is insolvent, *ie* has no assets with which to pay debts owed by the company. If it is, you are duty bound to declare the company insolvent and go into **liquidation**, which is the process used to wind up the business of a company.

You also owe a duty to the creditors of your company (*ie* businesses or individuals the company owes money to) not to continue trading when there is no reasonable prospect of avoiding liquidation.

If the company goes into insolvent liquidation the liquidator may apply to the court if he can prove that you knew, or ought to have known, prior to the liquidation that the company could not avoid taking that course. This is known as **wrongful trading**.

In these circumstances the court would make you personally liable to contribute to the company's assets and disqualify you from being a director again for up to 15 years. You will not be liable, however, if you can show that you have taken every step, prior to liquidation, to minimise the potential loss to the company's creditors.

Further if you knowingly intended to defraud your creditors it is **fraudulent trading**. You may still be expected to contribute to the assets of the company but may additionally be fined or even imprisoned.

> **It is your job as a director to see that your company can pay its debts and therefore avoid being accused of wrongful trading.**

COMPLETING YOUR ANNUAL RETURN

It is the directors' responsibility to see that the Annual Return (Form 363a, see Figure 9) is sent to the Registrar on time. It is now customary for the Registrar to forward to the company a Form 363s completed with the information he currently has on his file. This is known as a **shuttle annual return**. Any alterations to this information have to be completed before signing and dating it and sending it back. This makes it very simple.

The annual return contains the following information:

◆ the address of the Registrar
◆ the company number
◆ the company name

363a

Please complete in typescript,
or in bold black capitals.

Annual Return

Company Number 2958141

Company Name in full $SINCLAIR \ BROOK \ LIMITED$

Date of this return *(See note 1)*
The information in this return is made up to

Day	Month	Year
30	11	0X

Date of next return *(See note 2)*
If you wish to make your next return
to a date earlier than the anniversary
of this return please show the date here.
Companies House will then send a form
at the appropriate time.

Day	Month	Year

Registered Office *(See note 3)*
Show here the address **at the date of
this return.**

$5 \quad RIDGE \ PLACE.$

*Any change of
registered office
must be notified
on form 287.*

Post town $WARE,$

County / Region $HERTS.$

Postcode $SG51 \ 2PY$

Principal business activities
(See note 4)
Show trade classification code number(s)
for the principal activity or activities.

7011

If the code number cannot be determined,
give a brief description of principal activity.

Companies House receipt date barcode

When you have completed and signed the form please send it to the
Registrar of Companies at:
Companies House, Crown Way, Cardiff, CF4 3UZ   **DX 33050 Cardiff**
for companies registered in England and Wales
or
Companies House, 37 Castle Terrace, Edinburgh, EH1 2EB
for companies registered in Scotland   **DX 235 Edinburgh**

Form revised March 1995

Page 1

Fig. 9. Annual return to Companies House (page 1) (Form 363a).
(There are further details to be completed on subsequent pages of this form.)

- the type of company (e.g. private company limited by shares)
- the date up to which the return is to be made
- the address of the registered office
- the trade classification (identifying the principal activity by a code number)
- the address where the Register of members is kept
- the name and address of the company secretary
- a list of the directors showing, in each case, their name, address, date of birth, nationality and occupation
- details of the shares issued showing the class, the number and the nominal value
- a list of the members (*ie* shareholders) which contains names, addresses, number of shares held and dates of transfers if any.

The form, which can be signed and dated by a director or the secretary, is then sent, together with a cheque for £15 filing fee, to the appropriate Registrar.

There is provision on the Annual Return for any alteration in circumstances of directors like a change of address.

Case study: Hannah and Usha fix their dates

Diamond Designs Ltd was incorporated on 13 November, but Hannah and Usha realise that if the company's year end were to finish on, say, 30 November, that would also be when they hope to be at their busiest, selling hard for the Christmas trade. They decide to opt for 30 June as this will mean dealing with their year end during July and August which are their quiet months. Hannah, as company secretary, sends off Form 225(1) changing the date to 30 June.

FILING YOUR ACCOUNTS

All companies have to keep accounting records and each financial period, normally a year, must send their accounts to the Registrar of Companies.

Accounting reference date

The first accounts of a company start with the date of incorporation and run to the accounting reference date, which is the date decided by the company and which is the most convenient for their year to end (for example, 31 December).

The accounting reference date is chosen by sending to the Registrar Form 224 (see Figure 10) within nine months of incorporation. If you fail to choose a date the Registrar will choose one for you. It will be the last day of the month of the anniversary of incorporation.

A company may make up its accounts to a date seven days either side of the accounting reference date which may be useful, for example, for a retail shop which wishes its year to end on a Saturday. The period ending on the accounting reference date must be more than six months and less than 18 months.

You can change the accounting reference date within limits on Form 225(1). This notifies the Registrar that you wish to shorten or extend the current period and will state the new date. But you cannot:

- extend it to more than 18 months
- extend it more than once in five years.

Note that where companies own other companies or a company is directed to by the Secretary of State these rules may be altered.

G

COMPANIES FORM No. 224

Notice of accounting reference date
(to be delivered within **9 months** of incorporation)

224

Please do not write in this margin

Pursuant to section 224 of the Companies Act 1985 as inserted by section 3 of the Companies Act 1989

Please complete legibly, preferably in black type, or bold block lettering

To the Registrar of Companies
(Address overleaf)

Company number

2958141

Name of company

* insert full name of company

. SINCLAIR BROOK LIMITED

gives notice that the date on which the company's accounting reference period is to be treated as coming to an end in each successive year is as shown below:

Important
The accounting reference date to be entered alongside should be completed as in the following examples :

Day	Month
3 1	1 2

5 April
Day	Month
0 5	0 4

30 June
Day	Month
3 0	0 6

31 December
Day	Month
3 1	1 2

‡ Insert Director, Secretary, Administrator, Administrative Receiver or Receiver (Scotland) as appropriate

Signed *K. Brun* ‡ Designation ‡ **SECRETARY** Date **5ᵀᴴ APRIL 200X**

Presentor's name address telephone number and reference (if any) :

For official Use	
D.E.B.	Post room

Fig. 10. Notice of accounting reference date (Form 224).

94

> The Registrar will reject your company's accounts if
> they are made up to a date which is more than seven
> days before or after the accounting reference date.

The accounts

All limited companies must send their **Directors' Report
and Accounts** to the Registrar of Companies. This must be
done within ten months of the accounting reference date and
a new company must send its first accounts within 22 months
of incorporation.

Your accounts have only to be approved by the directors and
signed by one of them. They do not have to be laid before a
general meeting of the company's shareholders nor do they
have to be agreed by the Inland Revenue. They should be on
white A4 paper with black print.

The Directors' Report must be signed by an officer of the
company (director or secretary) and the Auditor's Report
must state their name and be signed by them.

The accounts include:

- a profit and loss account (or income and expenditure
  account if the company is not trading for profit)
- a balance sheet
- an auditor's report
- a directors' report.

Small companies

There are special rules which govern the way a small company deals with its accounts. To be a 'small company' it must

meet two of the following three criteria:

1. Its sales must not exceed £2,800,000.

2. Its balance sheet total must not exceed £1,400,000.

3. Its number of employees must not exceed 50.

Small companies may send abbreviated accounts to the Registrar which consist of an abbreviated balance sheet and a special auditor's report. Above their signature the directors must make a statement saying that they have relied on the exemptions for individual accounts on the grounds that the company is entitled to the benefit of those exemptions as a small company. The special auditor's report should also state that the requirements for exemptions are satisfied.

In these cases a full set of accounts, with a full audit report, must still be provided for the company members.

The audit

Small companies need not necessarily have an audit. The regulations for exemption are set out in Chapter 7. However, an audit can be demanded by a member holding more than ten per cent of the shares.

Where the company is eligible (*ie* it has a balance sheet total of not more than £1,400,000) and audited accounts are not needed, the balance sheet signed by the directors must contain statements that:

1. The directors are of the opinion that the company is entitled to the exemption from audit conferred by section

249A(1) of the Companies Act 1985;

2. No notice from members requiring an audit has been deposited under section 249B(2) of the Companies Act 1985, and

3. The directors acknowledge their responsibilities for:
    (a) ensuring that the company keeps accounting records which comply with section 221 of the Companies Act 1985, and
    (b) preparing accounts which give a true and fair view of the state of affairs of the company as at the end of the financial year and of its profit and loss for the financial year in accordance with the requirements of section 226, and which otherwise comply with the requirements of this Act relating to accounts, so far as applicable to the company.

Although you can see it is possible not to have an audit it is preferable as accounts are often used by third parties to assess your business. They are comforted by a clean auditor's report and the Inspector of Taxes also prefers it. It will cost more however.

A typical auditor's report where there is no audit undertaken might say:

'As described on the Balance Sheet you are responsible for the preparation of the accounts for the year ended . . . ., set out on pages . . . ., and you consider that the company is exempt from an audit and a report under section 249A(2) of the Companies Act 1985. In accordance with your instructions we have compiled these unaudited accounts in order to assist you to fulfil your statutory responsibilities from the accounting records and information and explanations supplied to us.'

You can see what it means to say the directors have the responsibility for the accounts when no audit takes place.

Harry opts for an audit

The management company is likely to have many different shareholders as people move on to live elsewhere and others take their place. Harry believes it is important that everyone involved is happy that the finances of the company, which they will all be contributing to, are seen to be above board and properly checked out. He asks a firm of auditors, different from the auditors who deal with his own affairs, to become advisers and auditors to Smiths Towers Management Co Ltd. In this way all the tenants will feel that matters are being independently checked.

NOTIFYING CHANGES IN YOUR COMPANY SET UP

At the beginning of this chapter there was a list of six changes that must be notified to the Registrar of Companies. There are many more but set out below are some of the ones applying to a small company. The forms have time limits on when they should be sent in.

Occurrence	Time limit	Form
Change of directors	14 days	Form 288
Change of secretary	14 days	Form 288
Change of registered office	on application	Form 287
Mortgages and charges	21 days	Form 395
Alteration to Memorandum and Articles	15 days	Copy of the resolution

| Liquidation | 15 days | Copy of the resolution |

It is a requirement that many important occurrences have to be notified and you would be well advised to seek professional advice when making any fundamental changes to the structure of your company.

Avoiding penalties

Remember to avoid penalties:

- send in forms within the time limit
- all forms must have original signatures and be dated
- forms and accounts must be in a form approved by Companies House and be clear and legible.

ACTION POINTS AND REMINDERS

1. You do realise that there are a number of responsibilities that you as a director of a company have and that there are fines for not carrying them out.

2. Certain basic forms must be submitted to the Registrar of Companies each year and you should know what they are.

3. The forms must be sent to the Registar of Companies.

4. When you hand over the job of completing the forms to your accountant it is still you who is responsible for sending them in.

5. If you cannot pay the people you owe money to what should you do?

6. The Registrar makes it easy for you to send in your annual return by completing it with the information he has on file. You only have to amend it if necessary.

7. Make sure your accounting reference date is suitable for your needs.

8. Your accounts should be sent in to the Registrar of Companies with the Annual Return.

9. You do not necessarily have to have an audit.

$$\binom{6}{}$$

Preparing for Business

Before you embark on any business venture you must prepare the ground. It is important to cultivate an image which will leave a lasting impression on the people you deal with. This chapter sets out the important elements of the preparation necessary for success. They include:

- choosing your name
- opening your bank account
- employing your staff
- equipping your business
- getting your message across.

CHOOSING YOUR NAME

If you have already started your business you may well have decided on a name. This may be your own name or one you have given it. It is a good idea to choose the name with care. Your future marketing may be helped or hindered by the name you choose.

For example, let us suppose your name is John Nelson, you live in Brockenhurst and you are starting a business as a printer. You have an infinite number of options for naming your business. Here are a few:

- John Nelson Printers Ltd
- J N Printers Ltd

- Nelson Printers Ltd
- Brockenhurst Printers Ltd
- Masterprinters Ltd.

Now consider some advantages and disadvantages of these names.

'John Nelson Printers Ltd' immediately identifies the business with you. This is useful where the people you deal with know you. If they do not know you then 'J N Printers Ltd' is just as good. 'Nelson Printers Ltd' also identifies you and is shorter and easier to remember whereas 'Brockenhurst Printers Ltd' lets people know where the business is situated. Unless you later move but cannot find premises in Brockenhurst! 'Masterprinters Ltd' is a description of what you do but does not say who or where it is.

Imagine also your business expands in the future and you wish to move your works or open another branch in, say, Winchester. The identification with Brockenhurst then becomes a liability as Brockenhurst is no longer the home of the business.

So you see it is worth taking a little time in deciding what your business name is going to be. And remember to check with Companies House that the name you want is available. For full details of requirements you may need to refer to the Business Names Act 1985.

OPENING YOUR BANK ACCOUNT

It is essential for a business to operate its financial transactions by using a bank account. This has a number of advantages:

- It is a permanent and independent record of your transactions.
- It provides a place to put your money until it is needed.
- It enables you to get rid of excess cash if you are in a cash business.
- It allows you to pay the people you owe money to conveniently and efficiently.
- It enables you to secure a loan or an overdraft when this is necessary.
- It gives you access to a range of other services.

Banks, like any other business, are keen to get more customers. If you are starting a new business there is every chance that most banks will be offering generous terms for you to join them. For example, they may offer free banking for the first twelve months of trading. This will normally be only if you remain in credit, that is if you have some money in your account all the time.

> **Shop around and see what all the banks have to offer before settling on one bank.**

Bank managers are human despite what some people may say. They are in business to make a profit just as you are and they want to see a sound business idea before they think of risking their money.

So if you are going to see a bank manager make sure you have done your homework first. He is interested in what you are going to do, where you are going to do it and how much money you are going to need to carry it out. These objectives must be clear in your mind.

Questions you should have answers to

♦ What will happen if your idea doesn't work?
♦ What will happen if you do not get the sales you expect?
♦ How much money will you be putting into the business?
♦ How much do you expect to take out regularly to live on?

Be the master of the facts and give your bank manager the confidence that you really know what you are talking about.

Opening a company bank account

As with most things these days you will have to complete a form. This will probably be in some detail as the bank will be contracting with the company and not you as an individual. They must get all the information they can.

General information required will normally be:

♦ name of the company
♦ company number
♦ registered address, telephone number, *etc*
♦ date of incorporation
♦ date of financial year end
♦ approximate expected turnover
♦ names, addresses, and details of directors and secretary
♦ address where the account will be run from (if different from the registered address) and where statements should be sent
♦ number of cheque books and paying in books required.

In addition the bank will require a bank mandate (see

Figure 11). This document will specify that on a certain date the directors held a meeting of the board and decided to appoint a particular banker. It also decided that the signatories were to be, say, any two of the directors and the secretary. This mandate would be signed by the chairman of the meeting. It would also contain specimen signatures of the people designated to sign on behalf of the company.

Once these formalities are completed the bank will open the account for business transactions.

Case study: Harry changes banks

Despite his reputation with his bank he finds they are not particularly interested in his management company as shortly he will not be a part of it when the tenants take over completely. In the interest of the new shareholders he contacts all the well known banks and secures a suitable account with an interest bearing deposit account attached and minimal charges for a minimal number of transactions. It is ideal.

EMPLOYING YOUR STAFF

You will recall that earlier it was seen that all the people who work for a company are employees. That includes the directors and the secretary. However, a new company may find it necessary to employ a member of staff, if for example the principal director feels he must be out selling and working and needs someone by the telephone to take orders and messages and do some office work.

The most important consideration is to pick the right person for the right job. Any employee incurs some basic costs including:

Name of company   SINCLAIR BROOK LTD.

Company's registered number   2958141

At a meeting of the Board of Directors on   Day Month Year   01 08 0X

It was resolved that Barclays Bank PLC ('Barclays')   Tick one

be appointed as our bankers ☑
New customers only

cancel all existing mandates given on our behalf except in relation to items and instructions dated prior to Barclays' receipt of this mandate, in which case our previous mandate will apply ☐

Barclays is authorised to

· debit our accounts with cheques, payment orders and bills of exchange, and
· comply with instructions, including those relating to safe custody items

whether or not our accounts become overdrawn or overdrafts are increased by doing so, and provided that such items or instructions are signed on our behalf by

ANY TWO DIRECTORS

Specify the positions of the persons who are to sign (not personal names) and in what combination for example, Managing Director alone or any two Directors together

This mandate is to apply to all existing and future accounts that the Company maintains with Barclays, until varied by the Company

It is agreed that Barclays

· has the right to refuse to allow, or increase, overdrafts on our accounts, and
· may require additional documentation from ourselves for some services or facilities

We confirm that the above is an accurate statement of what was agreed at the meeting

Signature of Chairman of the meeting   Signature of Secretary of the meeting

---

Name of company   SINCLAIR BROOK LTD.

Company's registered number   2958141

Account number(s)

Date   Day Month   01 08 0X

Cheques and other documents to be signed by   ANY TWO DIRECTORS

Specify the positions of the persons who are to sign (not personal names) and in what combination for example, Managing Director alone or any two Directors together

Please complete lists of approved signatures on both parts of the form overleaf

🦅 **BARCLAYS**   2

Fig. 11. Example of a bank mandate.

◆ wage or salary
◆ employer's National Insurance contributions
◆ possible commission or overtime.

You must therefore make sure the company can afford to pay such a person. And if so how much.

Deciding who you should look for

Some other considerations to take into account are:

◆ Is there a real job to be done?
◆ Could a temporary do it?
◆ Prepare a job description detailing the duties of the job.
◆ Decide where they are to come from. It could be a recruitment agency, advert or simply a suitable member of your family or a friend. (**Remember that you must not discriminate on grounds of sex, race or marital status in advertisements, interviews or job descriptions**.)
◆ Do they need to drive?
◆ Do they need any training?

Now when taking someone on you should be careful to start the relationship properly. You must:

◆ Tell the tax office when you take on an employee. You should get a P45 setting out the tax details of any previous employment from your new employee. If this is not produced complete a Form P46 and send it to the tax office instead.
◆ Present the employee with a contract of employment, *ie* a written statement, setting out the terms upon which they are employed.

Understanding the contract of employment

It is possible to make a contract with an employee verbally but there would be no permanent record so you would be well advised to make it in writing. It should contain:

1. An offer of employment from the company.

2. An acceptance of that employment by the employee.

3. The pay rate.

4. Anything else that makes up the terms.

If the contract is in writing it must contain:

- your company name
- the employee's name
- the job title with a brief description
- when the job began
- the place of work
- the rate of pay and when it will be paid
- the hours of work
- details of holidays, public holidays and holiday pay
- details of any pension scheme
- details of sick pay and how it is calculated
- the length of notice to be given by both you and your employee.

The employee must also be given the name of the person they should report to if they are dissatisfied with a decision or have a grievance.

As an employer you are required by law to deduct tax and national insurance from an employee's pay and account for the collection of it to the government. You must also broadly pay equally to any employees carrying out similar work or work of equal value. And you must pay statutory sick pay or maternity pay if it is due.

You must operate the PAYE system. The tax office will send you complete details of how this works.

There are many pieces of legislation relating to the employment of staff which are too numerous to cover in detail here. They include the discrimination laws, health and safety, minimum wage, maternity, part time work and employees leaving for whatever reason.

The subject may seem daunting but generally speaking you can employ whoever you want to and get rid of them if they are incompetent. But you must be reasonable and give them every chance to explain their actions.

EQUIPPING YOUR BUSINESS

There are three aspects to think about when considering the equipping of your business.

Deciding what equipment you need

This will depend on the type of business. If you intend to manufacture, machinery will probably be specific for your needs. If you are starting a service business you may only need office equipment. There are some types of equipment which will be common to all businesses, *eg* your telephone and your computer. And your transport is very important.

Deciding where to get your equipment

Make sure you buy the right equipment for your purpose. There are many suppliers of all types of equipment so make sure you get the best deal. Decide whether new or second-hand equipment is more suitable. Be careful not to be caught up in any long term agreements with suppliers.

Deciding how to pay for the equipment

There are four ways to consider:

1. *Purchasing outright.* This may mean using the company's own money or borrowing it from a bank for the purpose. If you do the equipment belongs to you and will show as an asset on your balance sheet. However, you may be using money you can ill afford.

2. *Hire purchase.* This is a way of borrowing but the asset will not belong to your company until the end of the hire period. In all other respects it is the same as buying outright. Your asset will show on your balance sheet and the amount outstanding to the hire company will show as a liability.

3. *Leasing.* When you lease the asset does not belong to your company. It remains the property of the leasing company. It is a useful option when money is short.

4. *Contract hire.* This is a type of leasing normally used for, say, a fleet of vehicles where the actual vehicles are not specified but the use of an agreed number is. The hire price may well include maintenance as well.

The equipment your company uses may have an impact on your customers. An efficient telephone system will give your customers confidence, but an answerphone usually means you do not have the resources to employ a receptionist. Your car will usually say something about you, but if a car is too big or expensive it may indicate rashness in your purchase beyond your means. Decent office furniture may be more efficient but more expensive.

Weigh up your means and your needs and try to select a level of standard and price which is within your capability.

Case study: Diamond Designs opts for new equipment

Business has been brisk since the opening of the workshop and with the little money they have accumulated and the prospect of increased business Hannah and Usha decide to buy some new equipment. Most of what they have been using to date was the equipment they used for their hobby and it is not hardy enough for the commercial world where it is in constant use. Workbenches and specialised tools are expensive and to fund the complete outlay is beyond their means. They decide to replace their existing equipment with new. They contact the hire purchase companies for the best deal and intend to fund the deposit with their own money. They prudently keep their old equipment as a backup.

GETTING YOUR MESSAGE ACROSS

It does not matter that you have formed your company, opened your office, bought your equipment and stocked up if you cannot sell your wares. Your customers must know why they should come to you rather than your competitor. And this implies that you know precisely what you are trying to sell and where your market is. If not you don't really deserve to succeed.

Coca Cola have developed a means of selling which consists of continually putting their product before you on television, radio, hoardings, videos, advertisements and sponsorship. You are aware what their product is and what it is for. It is an excellent formula for success, but it is horrendously expensive.

Your job is to find a way of doing this for your product which is much cheaper.

Choosing your marketing method

There are a number of alternatives:

- advertising
- mail shots
- brochures
- leaflets
- demonstrations
- press releases
- directories
- exhibitions
- personal contact.

These will not produce sales unless they are specifically targeted to the potential buyers. And most of them will take longer to materialise than you hoped.

Indirect marketing
You can give an impression of your business in other ways than direct selling:

- Your car is always clean.
- Your letterhead is eye-catching and informative.
- Your telephone manner is welcoming.
- Your invoicing is efficient and correct.
- Your image is consistent.
- Your delivery is when you say it will be.

All this helps to create in your customers' mind a caring, thoughtful and efficient business.

What is the return for all this effort?
It should help your customers to identify your products or services. It should create a desire for them. It should spark them into action and it should improve your reputation.

It may take some time to build this but it is a long term strategy. Customers like consistency of performance.

Case study: Dean increases his sales

For some time now Dean has appreciated that he needs to spread the word about his business to a much wider audience. He plans an advertising campaign. He consults an advertising agency for ideas. They advise a corporate image which is recognisable whatever activity he undertakes. They help him design a logo which will appear on all his products as well as his letterheadings and all his advertising material. He decides to target all the 'do-it-yourself' shops and all the motor dealers in his area with security products for the home and for the car. His new logo is striking and the enquiries begin to come in.

ACTION POINTS AND REMINDERS

1. Make sure that the name you have chosen will be suitable when your business expands.

2. Check with Companies House that the name you want is available.

3. Have you received concessions from your bank as a new business customer?

4. It is as well to meet your bank manager as soon as possible.

5. Are you contemplating any employees? If so, obtain the employer's starter pack from the tax office.

6. Will you need to buy any equipment? If so, how will you pay for it?

7. Consider what you want your company image to be.

8. Think about how you could improve your corporate image.

7

Producing Accounts

Why is it that one of the most uninteresting aspects, except to someone with an eye for figures, of any business is keeping financial and other records? Most entrepreneurs will be much more interested in chasing sales or doing a deal with a supplier but it is a fact of life that records of all kinds are an invaluable tool to anyone in business. History tells us a lot about the future and helps answer a lot of questions. This chapter explains what record keeping is and does. It includes:

- keeping your books
- watching your money
- having an audit
- making losses
- judging your business.

KEEPING YOUR BOOKS

Running a business in the 21st century entails keeping control of the daily deluge of paper that hits your office desk. Letters, enquiries, bills, tax demands, junk mail, invoices and mail shots are among the many bits of paper that have to be dealt with.

> The first rule in any office is
> **be organised**.

You must develop, as quickly as possible, a routine which suits you.

It could be as soon as you get to the office check the answer-phone for important messages. Then open the post and sort it into piles covering sales, buying and accounts. Make all the urgent telephone calls. Start the day's work.

These priorities may change as the business grows but the important thing is to have a routine which ensures you cover all aspects of the business and nothing is forgotten. Don't let your office work drift into chaos. It can be fatal.

Book-keeping

Accounting records, or book-keeping as it is more often known, are an essential part of this routine and you must set aside time to deal with your accounts data on a regular basis. Good records are needed for a number of reasons including proof of what is in your accounts and what is going on in your business. You will be required by the Inspector of Taxes and the Registrar of Companies to produce accurate accounts and the records you keep will justify the figures contained in them.

The records you keep will depend on the business but all businesses have to keep records of their cash and bank trans-actions. The main requirement of these records is to let you know how much cash or spending power you have at any one time.

Recording debtors and creditors
If your customers do not pay you when you sell them goods

you will have to keep records of what people owe you and for how long. Similarly you may buy your stock or goods on credit so you will need to know how much you owe and by combining the records of monies in and monies out you should begin to forecast what money you will need and when. These records will also tell you what you have spent in total, what has come in and whether you are making a profit or a loss. The more sophisticated your records the more accurate will be your results but you should keep the records as simple as possible so that the information you get is what you want. It is no good hoping your business is successful. You must know.

If you have employees you must keep accurate records so that your duty as a tax collector for the government is properly fulfilled. This applies to VAT as well.

There may be many other records to keep. These include details of customers, suppliers and services you use. But all this takes time, a commodity which may be scarce when you start a new enterprise.

Keep your records simple.

There is not sufficient space here to cover the many ways of book-keeping and you would be well advised to seek the help of an accountant to set you up with the simplest accounting procedure for your business. For some businesses there are ready made systems and, of course, you may well be computer literate and wish to use ready made book-keeping packages.

Summary

- Keep your records simple.
- Remember the records must be accurate for the taxman and the VAT man.
- Be methodical.
- Control of your business will be difficult if your records are not adequate.

WATCHING YOUR MONEY

All companies can be considered purely in financial terms and it is in this way that effective control of what is happening is exercised. Once upon a time a businessman might have run his business with very few records and some even 'on the back of a fag packet'.

Today everything is much more sophisticated and it is therefore easier to watch what is happening to your money. For example, the banks produce statements showing all your transactions with them. Not only is their system foolproof as far as the bankings and cheques paid out are concerned but also they may be entering transactions initiated or agreed by you but not generated by you directly. They may be:

- standing orders, which are instructions to the bank to pay bills on a certain date in the month or year
- direct debits, which means your supplier supplies his goods and takes his money out of your account with your permission
- bank charges or interest payments which are in accordance with your agreement with your bank.

You will appreciate from this that your records may be out

of date until you have verified these amounts by checking against your own books. Equally you may have made payments to suppliers who, for some reason or another, have not paid your cheques in and so the bank has not yet reduced your balance with them.

It is therefore essential that you keep your own record of the exact amount you have in hand so that you do not breach your agreement with your bank and run into unauthorised overdraft problems.

You will also need to know how much money your customers owe for goods and services supplied to them but not yet paid for. This record is normally a **sales ledger** which will show, in respect of each customer, how many invoices you have sent them, how many they have paid for and therefore how many are still outstanding.

The same system can be used for the suppliers of goods and services to you.

With these records you now know how much you have, how much you owe and how much is owed to you. If you plot this you can forecast fairly accurately what your cash position is at any time and be able to manage your money so that you do not overspend. Bank managers will be impressed with you if you have that knowledge.

All these recording systems are designed to ensure that you do not run out of money. Remember that the VAT man, if you are registered, will need to be paid at some date in the future, as will the taxman if you have employees. You will also be required to pay the tax on your own income at a later date. These occurrences can all also be built into your cash planning. Finally with good records you will be better able to plan for the future. You will be able to assess:

◆ how much money is available for your advertising campaign
◆ how you will be able to afford some new equipment
◆ when you can have your new car.

Major projections and realistic estimates like these can only be done when the basic information is available. All good companies know their current financial situation.

Case study: Usha uses technology

Usha's husband Kalim is a computer expert and he persuades Hannah and Usha to invest in a ready made accounts programme for the personal computer Usha has at home. This programme will record all the financial transactions which take place as well as keep a sales and purchase ledger. It will also generate statistics about the business which will be a useful tool to monitor how they are getting on. Usha agrees to put the computer in the office, at an agreed value, so that it is available for use at any time. She remembers to add it to their insurance.

HAVING AN AUDIT

It is not necessary for a small company to have an audit or appoint an auditor. The stringent rules applying to small companies have been relaxed in the last few years and now if your company:

◆ has a balance sheet total of not more than £1.4 million

it may be able to take advantage of these new audit requirements. Small companies tend to have auditors who not only
audit the accounts of the company but very often help the
company to prepare them and assist with their book-keeping
and tax matters. However, the auditor must not take part in
the management of the company.

**Note that if ten per cent or more of the members of
the company demand an audit the company must
have one**.

A company's first auditor is appointed by the directors. He
holds office until the general meeting at which the first
accounts are laid before the members. From then on it is up
to the members to re-appoint the existing auditor or elect a
new one at each subsequent meeting.

However, a private company can pass a resolution not to lay
its accounts before the members in general meeting. If this is
the case the auditor has to be appointed or re-appointed at
another meeting within 28 days of the accounts being sent to
the members.

In addition a private company can pass a resolution dispens-
ing with the need to appoint an auditor every year. In that
case the auditor remains in office until removed by passing
another resolution.

What does the auditor do?
The auditor has a number of functions. He or she should
ensure that

- the company has kept proper accounting records
- the company's accounts are in agreement with them
- the accounts comply with the requirements of the Companies Act 1985 (amended by the Companies Act 1989)
- the accounts give a true and fair view of the company's affairs
- the information given in the directors' report is consistent with the accounts.

When he or she is satisfied with this he gives a report to the members stating his or her opinion of all the above mentioned items.

Who can be an auditor?

Only certain people can be auditors. They must be members of a recognised supervisory body and must hold a current audit practising certificate. The five recognised bodies are:

- The Institute of Chartered Accountants in England and Wales
- The Institute of Chartered Accountants of Scotland
- The Institute of Chartered Accountants in Ireland
- The Chartered Association of Certified Accountants
- The Association of Authorised Public Accountants.

You must make sure the auditor of your company is registered. If you are in doubt contact his professional body.

It is for the directors of the company, providing it meets the criteria for opting out of an audit, to decide whether to do so. If they do not decide to opt out then the company must have an audit.

Can an auditor resign?

An auditor may resign in which case he or she must explain the reasons to the company and he or she may be removed by not re-appointing or passing the appropriate resolution. Note that he or she may have an entitlement to damages if the appointment is terminated by the company.

Case study: Harry takes the simple way out

The management company only has a few bills, mainly for repairs and maintenance, and Harry is now wondering whether it is necessary to have an audit done at all. He speaks to his advisers who agree that he does not. However, he must prepare a set of simple accounts to present to the members showing them the financial position and send a copy of the balance sheet to the Registrar of Companies. The company itself will become 'dormant' which basically means it has no significant accounting transactions during the period. The necessary resolution is passed.

MAKING LOSSES

Nobody forms a company with a view to making a loss. But it happens.

A company can make profits or losses in three ways:

1. Through ordinary trading.

2. By capital gains.

3. On investment income.

It is not compulsory for a company to make a profit but it helps!

It is possible for a company to make a profit on accounts but make a loss for the purpose of calculating any tax payable. This may also apply the other way round. The method of calculating profits for corporation tax purposes is dealt with in Chapter 10.

Losses are basically the difference between income and expenditure where the expenditure exceeds the income for the period of the accounts. The accounts of a company must show the income and the expenditure which relate precisely to the period of the accounts.

Example
Accounts for the year 31 December 200X:

Income	£45,000
Expenditure	£55,000
Therefore loss is	£10,000

The losses amount to £10,000 but included in the figures for expenditure is £15,000 paid as a salary to a director. It is therefore arguable that the company made a profit of £5,000 before paying the director's salary. This would be true if it was a sole trader business, but in a company directors' salaries are a deduction from profits as directors are employees of the company. They cannot give their salary back.

It is possible for a company to make a loss on its trading activities but to make a profit on the sale of an asset, like a piece of land or equipment. Land and equipment are held for the long term and expenditure on them is not made for the current year only. However, when the asset is sold the precise profit or loss is crystallised in the current year. For both accounts and tax purposes all these losses and profits can be set off against one another.

Despite the above examples the object of being in business is to make a profit. Losses, however made, have to be paid for out of the capital in the business and will diminish the amount of money left to invest in future trading. Too many losses will starve the business of all its capital and the closure of the business will result.

Monitor your activities well and the problems caused by losses will be minimised.

JUDGING YOUR BUSINESS

The ability to know what is going on in your business cannot be emphasised enough. It enables you to plan your next moves using the experience of hindsight and gives you a clearer view of where the business is going.

This can be highlighted by producing regular, say monthly, figures. You should know your monthly sales figures and they should be broken down into products or types of sale. You can get from your books an analysis of what your expenditure is being spent on: wages, goods for resale, telephone, electricity and so on. All this information gradually builds a picture of what is happening. It shows up seasonal fluctuations. It shows what happens in the holiday month of August, when sales may be up if you sell ice cream or down if you sell overcoats. It shows what happens if the unexpected happens, like snow in August when overcoats are at a premium!

Eventually you may deem it necessary to produce a regular flow of information including a set of accounts each month which will keep you fully informed and enable you to forecast what will happen with more accuracy. You will be able to change direction with confidence if you think fit. You will be judging your business for yourself.

Armed with this information how much easier it will be to convince others that you know what you are talking about. You can visit your bank manager with your head held high knowing you can satisfy him or her with your answers. You are now in control of most events.

Case study: Dean wonders about his cash position

Although Dean has made good progress with his advertising campaign as many enquiries have come in, he is still a little worried about his cash position. The expense of the campaign is draining his resources as the orders generated are not for immediate delivery. He therefore feels he must limit the amount he is taking out of the company as salary. This will bolster the bank balance and he can always make up the amount later when business picks up.

ACTION POINTS AND REMINDERS

1. Remember to keep your office organised and tidy.

2. Establish the records you will keep.

3. Records of sales and purchases should be kept if both are on credit.

4. Initially keep only essential records and do not waste time on unnecessary information.

5. Regularly check on your cash position.

6. Will your company need an auditor?

7. If not who will prepare your accounts?

8. Have you got sufficient information to judge your business success?

9. Check to see if your company making a loss on any of its activities.

$$\left(8\right)$$

Raising Money

Raising money for your company needs much thought:

- What is the money for?
- How much do you need and how long do you want it for?
- Where can you get it from?
- What guarantee can you give that it will be spent wisely?
- What security have you got?

You also have to convince serious people that you really need the money and excite them into giving, investing or lending it to you. Be prepared to spend some time on this project. It may be the most important 'SALE' you ever make. So you must get it right.

This chapter covers the raising of money from a variety of sources and explains how to go about it. It contains details of:

- preparing your business plan
- dealing with your bank
- finding your sources
- borrowing money
- issuing more shares.

PREPARING YOUR BUSINESS PLAN

You cannot expect to persuade people to invest in the future of your business unless you have a clear idea of where it is going. You must have a prepared plan which you can explain to anyone interested in helping you. You often hear stories about people who start enterprises without planning them but in reality it does not happen. Whatever your idea is it will need to be thought about and that is the first stage of your plan. You must then go into more detail. Each step must be considered together with any alternatives until you are sure it will achieve the objective you are seeking.

So what is a business plan?

A business plan can be prepared at any time. It projects your business into the future and tries to forecast what will happen. But you must have firm objectives first. It is a financial model of the future as far as your company or business is concerned.

What will it contain?

Your plan should contain the following:

- your ultimate goal
- the products or services you intend to sell
- what you will charge for the products or services
- how you will promote the business
- where you think your market is
- who your competitors are
- how you intend to manage the finances
- calculation of your break even point, *ie* the smallest amount of sales which in theory produce neither a profit nor a loss
- details of premises, equipment, vehicles, *etc*
- staff details
- personal details

◆ a cash flow forecast of the expected movements in cash over the next one or two years.

You should write up this plan as logically as you can and then re-read it to see if you can improve it. The idea is to give the potential reader a realistic summary of the current position and an optimistic view of the future without being too over confident. Over confidence may lead to some scepticism by the recipient. When you are satisfied that the plan tells the story as you see it you must check that your cash flow figures are in accordance.

Remember

If you secure a loan on the evidence of your plan and it fails to live up to expectations you will find it hard to go back for a bit more.
The credibility of your plan will be in jeopardy.

Make sure you are totally familiar with all the aspects of the plan. You must expect to be questioned in depth about its contents.

Now you are armed with a reliable business plan you can face possible lenders of money with confidence.

Case study: Hannah prepares a business plan

Hannah and Usha are getting very busy and realise that they will soon be working more hours than there are available. They agree to take somebody on to teach their trade to, but this will take time and therefore money. Hannah remembers from her studies that businesses should have a plan so she volunteers to prepare a plan of where the business is going and what funds will be needed to achieve it. She contacts the bank manager who sends her an outline plan which she works through, answering all the questions on the form. When this is complete Usha puts the finished product on the computer so that any adjustments that might have to be made can easily be done and for reproducing it when it is needed. A very useful job done.

DEALING WITH YOUR BANK

Your bank manager is only human. If you are a responsible businessman your bank manager will look upon your request for money with sympathy. Conversely if you upset your bank manager you will be treated accordingly. In business everyone is your friend whether you like them or not. You never know when your paths will cross again.

Anyone starting in business is naturally optimistic, but be careful when raising money not to ask for too much. You may overdo it. On the other hand if you ask for too little your business may not be viable. Try and be firm that the money your plan suggests is correct. Your bank manager may try to persuade you that you can manage on less but if you have done your homework properly you will be able to argue for the deal you want.

Financing your set-up plans

Your plan and forecasts will indicate how much money you want and when. If you are starting your business from scratch you will need money initially for setting up. This may include expenditure in two main areas:

1. The **initial expense** of buying equipment, premises, marketing costs and legal and professional charges.

2. **Working capital** which is the money you need to pay for your goods or stock prior to selling them and receiving payment. A number of factors affect the amount of working capital a business needs, including the amount of credit you give your customers and the amount your suppliers give you. You will need more if you hold large stocks.

Your bank manager has two main ways of funding your business: overdraft and loan.

Overdraft

Firstly you may be granted an overdraft facility if your need for money is likely to be short term. This means you will be able to draw more money out of your account than is in there up to a certain limit. The account is run as if it were your money and a charge for the interest you have incurred is debited to your account periodically. These interest rates may vary as interest rates have a habit of doing. It will be assumed that you will repay the outstanding sum fairly quickly.

Loan

Alternatively you may be lent money by way of a formal loan for a given period with regular repayments of both capital and interest. This may be used where larger sums are involved or where the money is required over a longer period. The rate of interest can be a fixed percentage or a variable one which will fluctuate with the movement of interest rates generally. There are a number of other variations of repayment and interest which can be negotiated.

Small Firms Loan Guarantee Scheme

This is a government scheme to help small businesses with no track record or security. The government guarantees a substantial part of your loan for up to £100,000 or £250,000 in the case of established businesses with two years' trading experience. There can be a holiday of up to two years before you repay any capital and the loan is repayable in full over a period of two to ten years. You can choose a fixed or variable rate of interest. The cost of this is that you pay a premium to the government on top of the interest set by the bank. There may be a charge from the bank for setting up your facility and you must remember that this amount will be charged to you at the time. It will effectively increase your borrowing. You may also be required to take out an insurance policy covering the amount of your loan should anything drastic stop you from fulfilling your obligations.

One other important consideration is that of **security**. A bank may well require, with certain types of loan, security which will give them the right over, for example, an asset of yours should you fail to repay your loan in accordance with the predetermined agreement. If it is the company which is doing the borrowing it may have no assets and the bank may require a personal guarantee from you that you will make the repayment should the company fail to do so. In each case this defeats your limited liability as you take on the debt personally under this agreement. You should consult your family before taking this step as they have a stake in your personal assets.

To summarise, the first impression you give may be vital. Make your plan readable but concise. Practise delivering your plan and remember you are normally dealing with fairly conservative bank managers. Don't be too outrageous yourself. If you are asked for more information get it organised quickly. Above all be yourself.

FINDING YOUR SOURCES

Banks are not the only providers of funds for new or small businesses by any means. There are many other sources. It is as well to investigate all these before you make any decisions.

Potential sources

- your own family
- your shareholders (this will be dealt with later in this chapter)
- venture capital companies
- hire purchase, leasing and finance companies
- individuals with capital they wish to invest
- local authority grants or premises
- Training and Enterprise Councils
- government loan guarantee scheme
- charities like the Prince's Youth Business Trust
- competitions, such as Livewire, for young people
- newspapers advertising competitions run by accountants, banks, *etc*.

Get in touch with as many of these as you can and show them you are interested. If you don't ask you don't get!

Most of these funders will require your business plan so have copies available. Their individual requirements may be different but your plan will be the basis for all of them. All the criteria for impressing your bank manager will apply to any of these funders so you must humour them. Imagine what you would be like if it was your money you were lending to someone else.

Case study: Harry doesn't worry

Harry has no cash worries in his little company as he can fund it from his own resources if necessary. It is a nice position to be in but he may well have to lend money to the company to tide it over until there is a full complement of shareholders. He will not charge any interest.

BORROWING MONEY

Borrowing money is never easy. Although you know what you want it for you will find the prospective lender sceptical, especially if you are just starting in business and you have a small company. The better your track record, the greater the chance of obtaining funds.

You will also find that lenders always like to see you put your own money into your enterprise. This gives them confidence that you are confident. Banks will often match the money you put in but are reluctant to put theirs in without some security.

Should you ask for more or less than you need?

Some people suggest that when borrowing money you should always ask for more than you need so that you can do a deal at the figure you really want when your lender beats you down. Others suggest you should be conservative. There are drawbacks in both of these approaches. The prime one is that your plan will have to be adjusted to agree with your request and this might throw your projections out. Of course if you ask for too little and get it you are going to run into difficulties when the money runs out and you are forced to go back for more.

The sensible course is to be realistic, have confidence in your figures and be firm in your negotiations. You know more about your business proposition than your lender so use the knowledge to your advantage. You will be respected all the more for it.

In the event of failure

If you fail to convince anyone to lend you money do not despair.

1. Look at your plan again.

2. See if you can adjust it.

3. Do you need all the equipment at once?

4. Can the purchases be staggered?

5. Are there alternative premises?

6. Are your sales too optimistic?

It is important to keep improving your plan until your lender can see it will work. Go through the whole exercise again until you are sure you are on the right lines. You will be learning all the time and there is no substitute for experience. If you have a good product there must be a combination that will work.

Case study: Dean runs short

Dean is having difficulty paying his creditors. He contemplates a visit to the bank to explain his predicament. He has a second thought. His father has some money and he asks him for a loan. His father is reluctant to take his money out of the building society as it is earning interest so Dean agrees to pay the interest as well at the same rate. However, there is a tax implication with this. Chapman Security Ltd will have to deduct tax at the basic rate (20 per cent in 1996) before paying over the interest. This will be shown on a certificate (form R185) to be given to his father at the time of payment. The company will subsequently have to account for the tax to the Inland Revenue on a form CT61 which is normally sent in quarterly.

ISSUING MORE SHARES

Mention was made earlier of raising money from your shareholders. This is always a possibility provided there are enough shareholders and that they have the resources.

Firstly you must make sure that there is sufficient un-issued nominal capital. If not, steps must be taken to increase it. Unless the Articles of Association say otherwise a resolution must be passed by the company in general meeting.

Example
'It was resolved that the capital of the company be and is hereby increased from £1,000 to £10,000 by the creation of an additional 9,000 ordinary shares of £1 each.'

A printed copy of this resolution authorising the increase must be filed with the Registrar of Companies within 15 days of the passing of the resolution. Also, as this is effectively amending the original Memorandum and Articles of Association, an amended copy of those must be filed.

Once there are sufficient shares to issue care must be taken to allot any new shares fairly. Consider this simple example.

Shareholders

	A	B
Shares already issued	600	400
Increase by 9,000 shares enabling £9,000 to be raised		
Allotted	3,000	6,000
New holdings	3,600	6,400

Shareholder A had 60 per cent of the original shares and therefore 60 per cent of the control. After the allotment of the new shares he only has 40 per cent and has lost control of the company to B. It is therefore important to allot these shares in the same proportions in which the holdings were originally held if a change in the control of the company is to be avoided. This may be difficult if the principal shareholder A has no money and B has. It would be better to try and negotiate a loan from B and leave the shareholdings as they are.

You must realise, therefore, that if you are willing to sell some shares to a third party you must first get the agreement of the other existing shareholders so that everyone knows the implications. You must relinquish some of the potential gains you might get as the value of the shares increases as your business grows. This after all is what any potential investor is looking for. And you will now have an additional person owning part of your company who may wish to exercise his or her power if events do not go the way expected.

Most small companies have a clause in their Memorandum and Articles which precludes shareholders selling their shares to anyone other than existing shareholders. So the market for shares is small and the value is restricted.

It may be better to pursue other ways of raising money first.

ACTION POINTS AND REMINDERS

1. Have you got a cash problem? If so try to identify it.

2. Have you got a future plan for your business?

3. Make sure your plan is written down.

4. Do you need some extra capital? If so when?

5. Approach your bank first and discuss the problem with them.

6. What are your alternatives?

7. Make sure you know your business well enough financially to give a good case to a lender.

8. What is your nominal and issued capital?

9. Will you need to issue more shares?

10. Who will buy them? And remember to watch the effect on the control of your business.

9

Using the Web

No book on setting up in business in the 21st century would be complete without a chapter on the World Wide Web. Many businesses have been taken by surprise at the speed at which the internet has intruded into our lives. And when you are in business you avoid the advantages of using the web at your peril.

This chapter looks at:

◆ Using the web for information
◆ Designing your web pages
◆ Marketing and trading on the web
◆ E-Mailing

USING THE WEB FOR INFORMATION

There is nothing worse than feeling left behind. So unless you are in the business of computers you may find the prospect of using the internet in business daunting. Admittedly it is a steep learning curve but a relatively short one.

The internet is an international computer network with answers to all the questions you may wish to know the answer to, with the ability to send messages across the world instantly, transfer documents, obtain supplies and technical information and generally do anything with numbers, words and pictures that you can do by any other means. In business it is becoming as integral as the telephone or fax machine.

Businesses are being set up at a very fast rate currently in a frenzy of activity so you will not be alone in using it as a business tool. But don't get carried away. It is essentiai to decide what your business can best derive from using the web.

The setting up of a limited company referred to earlier in this book can now be done on line. Company agents have web sites where registration forms can be filled in and the whole process completed without you leaving your computer. Sample memorandum and articles can be sent to you for checking that they adequately cover your needs. Names can be checked with the Registrar of Companies to ensure their validity.

The Companies Acts and other legislation can be accessed at any time to enable you to check that you are not acting outside company law. All PAYE and National Insurance rules and regulations are available on line.

Bank accounts may be opened on line and access to the details of your accounts can be made using appropriate security pin numbers. Monies may be transferred from one account to another and your accounts can be managed by you without the need to contact a person at the bank to do it for you.

As time goes by and security is improved you will be able to transact almost any business which requires data transference from the comfort of your own office.

One of the latest developments is the use of Broadband which enables you to access the internet through your telephone line whilst at the same time making normal telephone calls. This effectively gives you permanent access to the internet and is particularly useful where you need to obtain information rather send it. Your Internet Service Provider will give you full details.

DESIGNING YOUR WEB PAGES

The World Wide Web is the main commercial area of the internet used for selling, marketing and information about products and services but it is advisable to spend some time researching and getting to know how the internet works. Unless you have a brilliant and unique idea selling on the web involves hard and labour intensive work and small margins. You can, of course, design your own web page. This can be done with the use of special software but you may be well advised to use an expert. After all it is not putting your advertisement on line that is difficult but getting people to look at it. It may be wise to use the web as part of your promotion rather than rely on it alone.

Before you can do anything about designing your web pages you have to get your internet access provider to give you space on their hard disc. They usually give a small amount of space when they connect you and if you need more there will be a charge. Having published your pages and transferred them to your provider's site you must now hope that people will visit it.

Case study: Dean

Dean has always appreciated the need to market his products

well and has been using his computer for some time on his accounts. He has now registered with a service provider and intends to set up a web page for his business. He will use his existing logo and general corporate image to enhance the look of his pages but realises that he will need some training to get the best out of his site. He decides to enrol on a quick evening course at the local further education college which has a course on designing web pages.

Case study: Diamond Designs

The constant bombardment of www sites on television prompts Hannah and Usha to consider opening a web site to market their jewellery. Neither of them knows how to go about this but they are aware of the many advertisements for free access to the internet and decide to take advantage of one and explore the possibilities. They ring several free numbers for details and information packs. They are particularly worried about the cost of calls and who pays for them, They are also interested in 24-hour support which they feel they will need.

MARKETING AND TRADING ON THE WEB

You must make sure you know what you require the web to do for you. You may use it purely for customer awareness of your product. This can be as simple or complicated as you like. However if you intend to sell on the web then you must design how the customer will contact you. Orders can be completed on a form on line showing details of name, address, date required, products ordered and price. But to do this the range of products must be available to the customer with suitable references so that the correct product is sent out. The catalogue or list of products can be incorporated on the site but the more information you include the more it will cost to set up. It may also increase your rental of the site.

If you are selling on the internet your new customers will expect you to be carrying the stock to fulfil the orders. Your stock position is therefore very important and be aware that you may, if you are lucky, obtain a significant number of new customers. Failure to send out the goods could be detrimental to your business and gives the wrong impression.

You must also consider how goods ordered on line are to be paid for. Normal terms do not usually apply as you have no means of assessing your customer before you take him on. Payment in advance is preferable and this will probably be by credit card. You must see your bank manager to set up the system for receiving credit card payments.

E-MAILING

If you are looking for one good reason for using the internet look no further than e-mail. Once you are used to conversing by e-mail and have built up a suitable address book of all your contacts you will turn to it as your first line of communication.

You can send an e-mail to anyone in the world with an e-mail address of their own. It will enable you to write more letters, more often and get a response more quickly. In fact it is possible they could get your message quicker than you could print it. E-mail is always a local call and you can programme your mailreader to check for incoming mail at whatever interval you like.

E-mail is better than faxing as you never get an engaged

signal and you receive the actual text instead of a photocopy. As the image is original you can send messages in colour. You can send messages at any time, even when the recipient is in bed asleep and he or she can reply while you are asleep so that you get it in the morning. You do not therefore have to synchronise telephone calls and there are no answer-phones or receptionists to battle through. You cannot be put on hold. In other words you can, if you know his address, get straight through to the boss. But remember they can also get straight through to you.

There is another great advantage to using e-mail. You can attach a file to a message which means you can send pictures, spreadsheets, advertising material and many other documents or files and, because of this, your accompanying message can be brief and to the point. Business correspondence has, through e-mail, become much less formal and has got rid of the need for letterheads, logos, typesetting, signatures and deals only in words. It does mean you can deal with many more people than you otherwise would.

Incoming mail can be read at your leisure and can be answered immediately by returning the correspondence with your answer attached. Like a telephone call it is courtesy to reply quickly and you must be ruthless with deleting unwanted mail and filing only that which will be useful later. If a more considered reply is required then a quick acknowledgement is in order. It is possible to 'word process' your answer by using the text of the sender's message and inserting the answer immediately below it. This saves time and money and ensures accuracy.

E-mail can therefore be used for many of your communication needs and should be used for ease and speed. The finished product at the other end will not be as sophisticated as the printed word and or picture but where speed is essential it has no rival. And an attachment will solve the other problem.

Case study: Harry does not need a web site

Harry has access to the internet at his office and can see no reason to set up a web site for the company. All the shareholders are neighbours and e-mail is not necessary for communication. He asks his shareholders if they are personally on e-mail and is surprised to find they all are. This confirms that the facility is not required by the company.

ACTION POINTS AND REMINDERS

1 . Consider whether there is a commercial reason to be on the internet.

2. When constant and speedy communication is advisable the use of e-mail will be essential.

3. Check out service providers thoroughly before signing up.

4. Make sure you are aware of the costs involved both as monthly rental charges, if any, and telephone charges.

5. Find out what courses are available for training on web site design.

6. How will you make your web address available to your customers?

7. Do you intend to sell products on line? If so, suitable forms will have to be designed.

8. Remember to make reading of e-mails part of your daily routine as orders may be missed or messages not dealt with.

(10)

Troubleshooting

This chapter deals with the areas most companies and businesses have problems with. They are mainly things over which you have little control because you are dependent on others, but you must try to overcome them because they can be critical in your success. Points covered include:

- paying your taxman
- dealing with your creditors
- getting your money in
- insuring your problems
- training for your business.

PAYING YOUR TAXMAN

How often have you heard the cries 'I hate paying tax' or 'Why do I pay so much tax?' Well, the fact remains that all businesses have to pay tax and it is only *when* it is paid that differs. The main problem most businesses suffer, however, is having the money available to pay the tax when it is due.

Income tax

To recap, tax is, in theory, paid both by the company and its employees. Remember that directors are employees so the tax on all salaries and wages is payable under the PAYE (pay as you earn) system which is collected by you. The PAYE system gives you a code number which reflects the tax allowances to which you as an employee are entitled. Tables are provided by the Inland Revenue to convert the code into tax payable or repayable if you have paid too much. The income tax year starts on 5 April and both income tax and national insurance must be paid over to the Inland Revenue once a month. This tax is due to be paid by the 19th of the month and should include all deductions made during the previous month. The last date for sending payments for the year that ended on 5 April is 19 April and interest is chargeable on any payments made after this date.

> **It is important to pay your tax on time**.

When the tax year is over a return has to be sent to the Inland Revenue by 19 May showing the total amount deducted, the total amount paid and an explanation of any differences. This is called a P35. You are also required to send a form P14 for each employee showing his individual position. Finally by 6 June forms P9D and P11D must be submitted showing details of expenses and benefits.

You will see from the above that the taxman has a very foolproof method of collecting the taxes due from your company and if you are thinking about taking on employees you must be sure to have the wages and salaries system working properly. It sounds onerous but it is fairly simple and the starter pack issued by the Inland Revenue and the Department of Social Security explains exactly how to do it.

Corporation tax

Once you have ensured that your taxes in respect of employees are dealt with properly you have to deal with the tax bill on the company profits which is **corporation tax**. This was mentioned in Chapter 4.

The first thing to say here is that the Inspector of Taxes cannot know how to charge you corporation tax if it is not known what your profit is. The Inspector does, however, have a very effective way of ensuring that you pay it. In the past a letter was sent containing the assessment of your profit, either based on evidence of your profits in the form of your accounts or estimated. Since June 1999 it has been up to you to assess your own profits.

Don't panic. You must, however, deal with this promptly. It will be as well to learn how the system works. You will probably have appointed an accountant to deal with these matters, but that does not stop the taxman writing to you because you are responsible. Let your accountant deal with the taxman and don't get into the position where both you and the accountant do some of it. You can imagine the mess that will ensue if you both do something without the other knowing. Wires get crossed and the taxman has as much difficulty sorting it out as you do.

The important thing is to get your accounts done on time as the Revenue are imposing more and more penalties for late accounts.

Keep your book-keeping up to date

Firstly your book-keeping must be kept up to date. At the end of your financial year balance your books and seek the assistance of your professional accountant to prepare figures in a proper way which the Inspector will be used to. Profits are calculated for accounting periods which will coincide with your company's financial year end. You will be required to add back charges for depreciation and substitute capital allowances instead. You must also add back any business expenses which are not allowable (*eg* entertaining) and deduct any which are. If you should make a loss you have a choice of what to do with it. You can:

◆ deduct the loss from other current profits
◆ carry back the loss and deduct it from profits of earlier accounting periods
◆ carry it forward to deduct from future profits
◆ deduct it from investment income.

How much tax do you pay?

Once your profits for the accounting period have been determined you can calculate the tax to be paid. Rates of corporation tax are fixed for each fiscal year (6 April to 5 April). The tax is payable nine months after the company's year end under what is known as the **pay and file** system. At that point you are required to pay what you think you owe. Only when the Inspector and you agree the figures will a formal demand be made which will be after you have sent (filed) a corporation tax return. Again there are penalties for sending this in late. If the final demand differs from the amount you originally paid either there will be further payments to be made or there will be a refund. Both of these carry interest.

Finally if you are trying to minimise your tax bill you must pay yourself the amount at which the tax rate on your salary is equal to or lower than the corporation tax rate on the company's profits. After that the rate on your salary rises to higher rate tax. Don't forget that national insurance is also payable by your company on your salary.

The complexity of the taxation system in this country can only be touched on in a chapter like this so be guided by your professional adviser.

DEALING WITH YOUR CREDITORS

Your creditors are the people you owe money to at any time. You have seen how the taxman gets his money on time. Your bank may have a charge over assets of yours or a personal guarantee to force you to keep your debt to them under control. But the rest of your creditors have no such fallback position. They are in your hands as to when you pay them. They can, of course, withhold supplies to you, whether it is supplying no more goods or materials or cutting off your supply of electricity. However, the goods or services you have already consumed and not paid for are different.

You can manipulate your cash flow by planning the payment of your suppliers. If you hold up payment you increase your cash and if you pay too early you reduce your cash. Holding up payment too long may upset your supplier and make them reluctant to deal with you. Like most things it is a matter of confidence in one another.

Looking at your credit arrangements

Firstly you should check all the credit arrangements you have with suppliers. Can the terms be extended? Or are they, like you, trying to get their money in as soon as possible? If you say you will pay a bill next week, or worse say the cheque is in the post when it isn't, you may cause your creditor to panic and either stop supplies or more drastically issue a writ.

You see there is a fine balance to cope with and you may have to seek more permanent finance to give you the elbow room to deal with your creditors properly. If you have cash problems paying your creditors late is a short term way of dealing with it, but it is a very hazardous journey if you cannot contain it.

It is possible for a creditor to investigate your status as a company through one of the credit agencies set up for this purpose. They may initially ask you to pay in cash until you have a track record. Or they may ask for one or two trade references from other suppliers of yours. If your order is very large you may get asked for a set of accounts or even a personal guarantee like the bank does. All these measures are designed to safeguard their money as much as they can.

You will help yourself by having records which keep you informed of:

- the name of your creditor
- how much you owe
- how long you have owed it
- your record of business with them.

Then establish a pattern of paying your bills, say, once a month. This creates a continuity which gives your supplier confidence and gives you the excuse that you only pay your bills at the end of the month.

Above all be honest with yourself and make your plans accordingly.

GETTING YOUR MONEY IN

Roughly the same things apply to getting your money in as to paying your creditors. The big difference is that you will invariably be told by a supplier if you have not paid. The same cannot be said for everyone who owes you money.

The people whom you supply, your customers, are known as **debtors** and it is as well to formulate a system early on to keep track of what you are owed and keep it coming in. The following might be a plan of attack:

1. Make sure your customer knows your terms of credit.

2. Call or write, politely, as soon as he has gone past the date.

3. After seven days follow up with a fax or written letter making sure all the facts are correct.

4. After another seven days telephone to find out the problem. Are there queries on the account? Find out when they make their payments normally.

5. Keep ringing until you get a promise of payment.

> **Don't give up. Perseverance is the name of the game**.

6. If they will not speak to you try being someone else until you get the person you want. Pick your times carefully.

7. If they say the cheque is in the post, ask when it was sent, for how much and the cheque number.

8. Go and get the cheque yourself.

9. When you get the cheque bank it immediately, checking the details are correct.

10. If all this fails get on to your solicitor to start recovery proceedings. Take his advice with any further action.

You see the procedure to be adopted is one of continual pressure until you can establish an understanding with your customer which is acceptable to you both. The alternative is to stop supplying them.

Case study: Dean plans to get his sales money in

Dean has always relied on his knowledge of his business and particularly his customers when it comes to getting his money in. But as the business has grown he finds he can't remember the details. It is no good seeing a customer and saying to them 'How much do you owe me?' He decides that he must glean more from his sales ledger. He carries a list of monies owing to him wherever he goes and takes every opportunity to remind his customers what they owe. He institutes in his office a regular monthly statement to each customer showing their outstanding balance and when it is payable. He spends a morning each month telephoning his bad payers and ensuring that he finds out from them when the bill will be paid. He warns them that he will stop supplies if they do not respond. His cash flow increases.

Factoring

There is one other way of getting in your money. That is to sell your debts to raise cash. This is known as **factoring**. The factor takes over your records and collects your debts. He passes the money to you after having deducted his fee. This is only really a feasible method where your debts are considerable, say over £100,000.

INSURING YOUR PROBLEMS

Insurance is a necessary evil. Paying premiums to insurance companies to cover risks you hope will not happen anyway is not the most exciting job you have to do. But it is an important aspect of any company and should be taken seriously.

What risks should you cover?

Employers liability
Covers injury to an employee. A normal amount might be up to £2 million. A certificate must be displayed at the place of work.

Motor
Normally covers all vehicles for third party damage as well as damage to your own.

Machinery
Some equipment has to be covered by law for safety reasons, but it is as well to cover all equipment and machinery. This includes computers and other office equipment.

Fire
Covers buildings and contents against fire.

Theft
Covers burglaries and theft from your premises.

Loss of money
Where you handle significant amounts of cash, cover is available.

Goods in transit
When you deliver goods either in your own vehicles or by other carrier.

Credit
Against customers failing to pay. A good record of collecting your debts is essential to get this cover.

Public liability
Covers your liability to visitors or members of the public if you cause them injury or damage their property.

Professional indemnity
If your business entails giving expert advice you will be covered against claims by your clients for damages caused by negligence.

Keyman
If your business relies heavily on one or more individuals a life assurance policy will cover the death of one of them.

Personal
Make sure you are personally insured properly to provide for your family in the event of unforseen circumstances. This includes health and pensions.

Get yourself a good firm of insurance brokers and go through all these with them. You may find the cost of covering for all of them prohibitive but the broker will advise you on priorities in your company.

Case study: Hannah and Usha check their insurance

Diamond Designs had a break-in and although the intruders were disturbed they got away with some made up jewellery. Hannah checked the insurance. Their broker sent her a claim form as they were covered for theft, but she took the opportunity to check out the other insurance cover they had. As some people paid in cash would this be covered if it was stolen? They had no 'loss of money' insurance but this meant the installation of a safe. This would be useful anyway to keep finished jewellery in. The directors decided to have an adequate safe concreted in and to extend the cover to all items in the safe. The cost of this insurance was not prohibitive as they now have taken proper precautions to look after their property.

TRAINING FOR YOUR BUSINESS

You are never too old to learn, the saying goes, and that is as true of business as any other field. Training for business and knowledge of running a company can come in many ways. Some of these are:

- ◆ your friends in business
- ◆ professional advisers
- ◆ newspapers, books, television and radio, magazines
- ◆ exhibitions
- ◆ local business organisations (*eg* chamber of commerce)
- ◆ trade associations
- ◆ Business Links, TECs and Local Enterprise Agencies
- ◆ university and management training courses.
- ◆ the internet.

The list is endless. But where do you find the time? After all you might say 'I've got a business to run'. Like most other things you must set your priorities and plan to carry them out. Training should be one of them.

Anyone starting a business should go on some sort of management training course. No one is expert in everything and if you are good at your chosen trade you may not be good at book-keeping, for example. Some courses are general, giving the rudiments of a subject, and others are specialised, going into depth. Choose the one that suits you best.

Business Link

A network of Business Links has been established throughout the country designed to give information and advice to small businesses. There you will be able to get advice on courses. They will give you lists of courses available, whether they are on-the-job or classroom based, whether there are any training allowances available and the cost if any. There may be grants available or arrangements for business start-up. They will also provide facilities for business health checks, project management support and access to technology and design services. There is, therefore, together with the TECs and Local Enterprise Agencies (Trusts in Scotland), a wide range of information available to the small business and any budding entrepreneur would do well to consult with them and find out the many ways that they are able to help.

Case study: Harry arranges training

Harry was anxious to pass the running of the management company over to someone competent to do it. Most of the tenants had no idea how to run a company and he decided to contact the local Business Link to see what training was available. There he found a simple management training course for people starting in business and persuaded one of his tenants to take the course with a view to taking over the day to day operation of the company. He agreed to pay the fees and the tenant agreed to take the course. The course lasted six weekly evenings and Harry was able to hand over at the end of it.

Remember

◆ Seek help and assistance, much of it is free.

◆ Choose your courses carefully.

◆ Join a business club if there is one.

◆ Read avidly both trade and general literature.

ACTION POINTS AND REMINDERS

1. Save money regularly so that you can pay your tax when it is due.

2. If you have employees learn how the PAYE system works.

3. Get a supply of all the necessary forms from the Inland Revenue.

4. Make arrangements with your accountant to have your accounts prepared soon after your year end.

5. Check your own salary entitlement to the best tax advantage.

6. Make sure you have a suitable book-keeping system for paying the money you owe.

7. Make sure your money comes in regularly.

8. Check your insurance annually to see that all eventualities are covered.

9. Do you need any training?

10. Telephone the local Business Link for advice.

Closing Down

There are many reasons for a business ceasing to trade, but in a company this has to be dealt with according to the rules. In this final chapter the various reasons are discussed in some detail and include:

◆ ceasing to trade

◆ disposing of your business

◆ planning your retirement

◆ going into voluntary liquidation

◆ suffering compulsory liquidation.

CEASING TO TRADE

There may be circumstances where you wish to close down your company and trade no more. Your business may be becoming unprofitable or overtaken by modern technology. You may wish to sell the shares or the assets to a competitor or just to a younger person. You may not be able to pay your debts or you may wish to retire. The fact is that whether a company is a success or a failure it is up to you what you do with it if you hold the power in the shares you own.

When the company is sold the shares pass to another shareholder who takes on all the responsibilities you once held. On the other hand if you clear the company of its assets and retain your shareholding you may wish to end its existence. If the company cannot pay its way the law gives you no alternative but to do something with the company.

This act of extinguishing the life of a company is known as **liquidation** and the process may be either voluntary or compulsory. The difference is explained in some detail later in the chapter.

DISPOSING OF YOUR BUSINESS

It is, of course, possible to dispose of your company at any time. You may have found a suitable buyer, or another company who wants to take you over. You may wish to retire and sell your interest or you may want to pack up and go. Whatever the reason the disposal must be orderly and some statutory procedures have to be followed.

When you are selling a business you must establish whether you are selling the shares in your company or only the assets. A potential buyer may want to take your company lock, stock and barrel and either purchase the shares or use an existing company to buy the shares, in which case the company would be wholly owned by another company and become a subsidiary of it.

Case study: Usha is pregnant

Usha is expecting her first child and, after long discussion with her husband, decides that she must shortly stop working. This is a blow to Hannah, who is really a 'career girl', and the partners have to decide what to do. They could close the business down but that would waste the time and effort they have put in. They compromise and Hannah agrees to raise the money to buy Usha out of the business. The shares will have to be valued and Usha agrees to employ a separate accountant to negotiate the deal on her behalf. The company will remain in existence and Hannah will eventually become the sole owner of the shares and the business.

Selling the assets

It could well be more advantageous for a buyer to take only the assets you own and incorporate them into an existing business. This may or may not include the **goodwill** (which can usefully be described as the ability to make a profit). You would be left with the company liabilities to pay and the money paid for the assets you sell. On the other hand you may sell the whole business, including goodwill, for a given price and finish up with a company which contains only cash. Whichever way the sale goes you will have achieved your goal of selling and be left with the money in your company.

The next problem is to get the money out. It could be used to invest in another business run through the same company. However, if you wish to remove the money from the company inevitably the taxman is hovering around to take a share of the spoils. Tax is normally only payable if you realise the gain and take it away. You can also obtain some relief from inheritance tax if you give away business assets.

Selling the shares

There is relief from tax, at least for a while, if:

1. You sell shares in an unquoted company.

2. You have been a full-time working director.

3. You have owned more than five per cent of the shares for more than one year.

4.   You invest the money in another unquoted company.

If, however, you just wish to dispose of your shares and walk away you will be liable to capital gains tax on the difference between the value of the shares you bought and the value when you sold them. There is an indexation allowance for inflation during the period you held the shares. This is just like selling shares on the Stock Exchange.

You will qualify for concessions if you are 50 years of age or over and retiring as there are a number of reliefs available – for example, retirement relief. If you sell a business, give it away or sell off the assets after you have closed the business (for example, a family owned company) there will be relief if you owned shares in the business for more than one year.

The rules of taxation are somewhat complex and again you would be well advised to seek your accountant's advice before being too hasty with your disposal.

PLANNING YOUR RETIREMENT

It is never too early to plan your retirement, however far away it seems. You will spend most of your time ensuring your company will be a success. If, when you retire, you sell it you should have a handsome sum of money to invest that will provide you with an income to live on. But don't bank on it as it may not be worth enough when the time comes.

Very often you will have all the skills while you are working but when you leave the business there is no business left. On the other hand you may be forced to retire because of ill health.

What happens if your business is going through a hard time when you are taken ill? Or you suffer the ravages of inflation or recession? And what will happen if you just do not accumulate the amount of money you need to continue to live in the manner to which you have become accustomed?

The only way to alleviate this potential problem is to invest in a suitable **pension** arrangement.

The state pension

As an employee of your company you will be paying Class 1 contributions personally and the company will pay the employer's contribution. You may also pay additional contributions as an employee and this will entitle you to the State Earnings-Related Pension commonly known as SERPS.

Personal pension

You can, however, opt out, or contract out, of paying for SERPS and redirect the additional national insurance contributions to your own personal pension. There is a limit on pension benefits which is reviewed annually.

The type of personal plan you choose must depend on individual circumstances and there is a number of providers such as banks, insurance companies, unit trust managers or building societies. You must shop around to find the most suitable.

Types of plan
General types of plan are:

◆   *Unit linked* – where you choose how your money is invested whether property, shares, currency, government stocks or a combination of all of them. Your potential pension fluctuates with the value of the units.

- *With profits* – where the insurance company invests your money as it thinks fit. There will usually be a guaranteed pension topped up with bonuses as the value of the investments increases.

- *Without profits* – where the pension is fixed and you know when you start what it will be.

Case study: Dean thinks about retirement

Although Dean has cash flow problems all the time he still makes profits, a phenomenon he finds hard to understand. 'How can I make profits when I never have any money?' His accountant explains that his money is always tied up in stock and debtors and until he gets his system for realising his cash working better and sooner he will continue with the problem. Now the question is how to alleviate the tax on his profits. His accountant suggests, despite his young age, that he might like to start a modest pension scheme which will be wholly allowable against his profits for tax purposes. He agrees and finds himself discussing the proposition with an independent financial adviser recommended by his accountant.

Occupational pension schemes

You can also arrange an occupational pension through your company. It has to be approved by the Inland Revenue to qualify for tax concessions and may be administered through an insurance company or by administering the investments yourself. There are advantages to having such a scheme:

- there is no limit on the contributions and this enables you to put in much larger sums when business is good

- the fund can be used to provide the capital for buying premises or major items of capital expenditure
- up to half the fund can be loaned to the company.

This scheme is a specialised method of acquiring a pension and you will be well advised to consult your financial adviser before doing anything.

Tax reliefs

Any tax relief you receive will always be at your highest rate and, for example, if you are a 40 per cent tax payer it means that you will only pay £600 for every £1,000 of pension you invest in. It is indeed a bargain.

Remember

- Start your plans early, picking the most suitable plan for you.
- Take advice.

GOING INTO VOLUNTARY LIQUIDATION

A company may by resolution go into a **voluntary** winding up or liquidation. This may be done because the company is no longer required, because it is insolvent or likely to be or it may want to reform in a different way.

Members' voluntary liquidation

This winding up may be carried out by the members provided the directors are of the opinion that the company can pay all its debts within a period of twelve months. If so the directors call an extraordinary general meeting and make a statutory declaration of solvency. Once this resolution is passed a liquidator can be appointed. Within 14 days a copy of the resolution must appear in the *London Gazette* (the official announcement of such matters) and a copy sent to the Registrar of Companies. Also the liquidator must give notice of his or her appointment to the Registrar and in the *London Gazette* within 14 days.

If the directors make a statutory declaration without reasonable justification and the company cannot meet its debts, then they can be liable to fines or imprisonment.

The liquidator then uses his or her best endeavours to realise the company's assets, pay the creditors, clarify any claims on the company and distribute the funds. Their fees and expenses take priority over all other charges.

Creditors' voluntary liquidation

This will occur when the directors of a company are unable to declare their solvency. In these circumstances the creditors have a greater say in how the company will be wound up.

The directors first call an extraordinary general meeting to consider the winding up in the context of not being able to pay its creditors. Within 14 days of this meeting the directors must call a meeting of creditors and present them with a financial statement of affairs, verified by affidavit, and answer any questions put to them by the creditors. A liquidator may have been appointed at the first meeting and if so the creditors may approve the appointment or appoint another in his or her place.

The liquidator then takes control of the company and realises the assets. After his or her expenses he or she will distribute the funds available paying in the following order:

1. His/her own fees and expenses as liquidator and the costs of the liquidation.

2. The preferential creditors which includes monies owed to employees and any rates or taxes due.

3. The secured creditors – *ie* those creditors with a charge over certain assets of the company.

4. The unsecured creditors – *ie* the rest of the people to whom the company owes money.

5. The balance, if any, to the shareholders in the proportion of their shareholdings.

The liquidator's appointment must be advertised in the *London Gazette*, as with a members' voluntary liquidation, and notified to the Registrar within seven days. The creditors may appoint a liquidation committee to monitor the work of the liquidator and, if thought fit, to fix his or her fees.

The end of the road

In both cases on completion of the distributions the appropriate forms, including a receipts and payments account, are submitted to the Registrar by the liquidator and the company no longer exists.

SUFFERING COMPULSORY LIQUIDATION

There can be circumstances where a company is wound up by the court. These include, amongst other things, where:

◆   the company passes a special resolution to that effect

- the company does not commence business within a year, or suspends its business for a whole year
- the company is unable to pay its debts
- the court is of the opinion that it is just and equitable that the company should be wound up.

The procedure is started by those persons entitled to present a petition to the court. They include the company, the directors, a creditor or creditors, any shareholder or the clerk of a magistrates' court.

When the court makes the winding up order the **Official Receiver** becomes the liquidator of the company. The directors are required to submit a statement of affairs and be interviewed. The office receiver can then decide to call a meeting and ask the creditors and shareholders if they wish to appoint another liquidator instead. If the Official Receiver does not advise them of such a meeting 25 per cent of the creditors in value may require it to be done.

The liquidator, or the Official Receiver, will then carry out the liquidation of the company and realise and distribute the assets. The Registrar of Companies must be informed that a liquidator has been appointed and advertised in the *London Gazette*.

There is, however, usually a good reason why someone petitions to wind up a company and if fraud, embezzlement or any other crime where the directors are involved is suspected the liquidator must inform the Secretary of State for Trade and Industry and within six months produce the evidence for this. Equally the Secretary of State may have appointed

Inspectors to investigate a company on the grounds that it has been fraudulently mis-managed and may petition if he or she thinks fit.

Any company finding itself in this position probably deserves what it gets.

Case study: Harry remembers

Harry once got involved as a shareholder by putting £3,000 in a company in the building trade. The directors of the company had systematically milked the company of its money by doing jobs for cash and pocketing the money without accounting for it in the books. When Harry found out, which was only because the company was having great difficulty paying its debts, he decided to petition the court to wind up the company. A liquidator was appointed and Harry was required to give evidence. He had a good knowledge of the customers the company was building for and spoke to each of them to find out the financial position of each job. It was obvious all the money was not being accounted for properly and he had witnesses to prove it. The company was wound up and Harry lost his money.

ACTION POINTS AND REMINDERS

1. Remember if you want to sell your business, you can sell the assets without selling the shares.

2. If you want to retire, is there enough value in your business for you to retire on?

3. Have you got a personal pension arrangement?

4. Does your company have an occupational pension scheme?

5. If you want to close your company down make sure the reasons are clear.

6. If your company cannot pay its debts you must close it down.

7. You will be forced out of business if you don't.

Glossary

Accountants. Professional experts in finance, business purchase, accounting and tax.

Allotment of shares. The allocation of shares by the directors to the first shareholders of a private company.

Annual General Meeting (AGM). The annual meeting of a company which considers the accounts, the auditor's report, any resolutions, the appointment or re-appointment of directors and auditors, the proposal of dividends and any other general business of the company.

Articles of Association. The internal regulations governing the management of a company and the relationships of its members with each other and with the company.

Asset. Any item of value owned by a company.

Authorised capital. The amount of share capital, declared in the Memorandum, which the company is authorised to issue.

Balance sheet. A statement of the worth of a company at an accounting date.

Benefits. Amounts paid to employees of a company other than in money.

Broadband. Permanent internet access.

Business. Any entrepreneurial enterprise carried out in return for money or value.

Business plan. A plan prepared to convince others that a company is viable.

Capital. The value of the shares in a company.

Certificate of Incorporation. A document signifying that the members of a company have become a body corporate and statutory requirements have been complied with.

Companies Acts. Parliamentary legislation referring to the conduct and administration of companies.

Company. An artificial person or corporation created by law and endowed with perpetual succession, and existing apart from its members.

Company Registration Agent. One who deals in the formation of companies on behalf of customers.

Company secretary. The chief administrative officer of a company who has statutory recognition under the Companies Act 1985 and who has ostensible authority to enter into contracts of an administrative nature on behalf of a company.

Creditors. Those persons and corporate bodies that a company owes money to.

Debtors. Those persons and corporate bodies that owe money to a company.

Debts. Amounts owed to a person or corporate body.

Director. There is no statutory definition of a director but a director is one who acts as agent in any transactions entered into on behalf of the company and as trustee of the company's property and money.

Directors' report. The annual report of the directors to the members of their stewardship of the company.

Dividend. Amounts of profit paid to shareholders in proportion to the shares they hold.

Domicile. The administrative area, under the Memorandum, in which a company is based.

Drawings. Amounts of cash or worth withdrawn by its owner from a business which is not a company.

Emoluments. The remuneration, including any salary, fees, contribution to pension schemes, expenses chargeable to income tax or other sums, paid to a director.

Extraordinary general meeting. A special meeting for the purpose of putting extraordinary or special resolutions before the members of a company.

Finance Act. The Act of Parliament initiated by the Chancellor of the Exchequer covering financial matters and containing those parts of the Budget passed by Members of Parliament.

Firm. A collection of individuals bound in partnership for the purpose of carrying out a business.

Fringe benefits. See Benefits.

Goodwill. The added value which accrues to a business over and above the true net value of the net tangible assets by reason of its ability to earn profits in excess of normal profits expected from the risk capital and labour involved.

Issued capital. That portion of the authorised capital that has been subscribed for.

Joint shareholding. Shares owned by more than one person together as one holding.

Joint stock company. An incorporated company which could hold property and sue and be sued in its own name, but where the liability of the members remains unlimited.

Liabilities. Any money or money's worth owed to a person or corporate body now or in the future.

Limited liability. The restriction of the contribution of a shareholder to the nominal value of the shares he has purchased.

Members. Shareholders in a company.

Memorandum of Association. A registered document which defines a company's status, name and powers.

Nominal capital. See Authorised capital.

Objects clause. The clause in the Memorandum which sets out the purposes and powers of the company.

Off the shelf. A ready-made company from a company registration agent.

Paid up capital. That proportion of the issued capital that has been paid for.

Partnership. The relationship which subsists between persons carrying on a business in common with a view to profit (Partnership Act 1890).

Pay as you earn (PAYE). A scheme where employers have to deduct income tax and national insurance from employees' wages and salaries each month and pass them to the Inland Revenue.

Pension. An insurance arrangement to provide a fund out of which the subscriber will be paid during retirement.

Personal allowances. Amounts of income of an individual which are not subject to tax.

Profit. The excess of income over expenditure for a given period of time.

Profit and loss account. An account summarising the income and expenditure of a company and showing whether it has made a profit or a loss.

Proxy. A shareholder who is appointed by and acts and votes for another shareholder at a general meeting of a company.

Quorum. The number of people required to attend a meeting to make it valid.

Registered office. The official address of a company which has been submitted to the Registrar of Companies as such.

Registrar of Companies. The chief officer of Companies House, which is the executive agency of the Department of Trade and Industry, dealing with the incorporation, regulation and dissolution of companies under the Companies Acts and the provision to the public of information about these companies.

Remuneration. See Emoluments.

Resolution. The means of getting agreement to a course of events by the shareholders of a company.

Return of capital. The amount of profit generated by an asset or assets expressed as a percentage of the value of the assets.

Security. Assets put up as collateral or guarantee against loans.

Share. The title of ownership of a stake in a company.

Share capital. See Capital.

Share certificate. The document issued to a holder of shares in a company to prove entitlement to them.

Shareholder. The owner of shares in a company.

Sole trader. A self-employed proprietor of a business.

Solicitors. Those professional experts dealing with the law.

Special general meeting. A general meeting of the company called to consider any special resolutions brought before it.

Stock transfer form. The document which transfers shares from one member to another for value.

Subscriber shares. See Issued capital.

Surveyors. Those professional experts dealing with all matters in connection with property and land.

Training and Enterprise Councils (TECs). A nationwide network of centres under government guidelines to foster business enterprise skills.

Turnover. The aggregate sales of a company.

Unearned income. Income of an individual received from the ownership of shares.

Useful Reading

This book has been written as a guide to the entrepreneur who specifically feels the need to run a business through a company.

There are many books published on the various aspects of starting and running a business. These cover topics like:

Being your own boss

Business opportunities

Earning money from home

The first twelve months in business

Getting started

Home is where the office is

Preparing business plans

Small business finance.

The major banks also produce books and guides to help the budding entrepreneur and the *Daily Mail* has a guide to running a small business.

However, it is recommended, after studying this book, that further information is obtained for specific purposes from one of the organisations listed overleaf.

SOURCES OF INFORMATION

This list gives you contact organisations that can be of help to you. The addresses and telephone numbers, where applicable, will be found in your telephone directory or *Yellow Pages*, or may be contacted through Directory Enquiries.

ACAS
Accountants
Advertising Standards Authority
Association of Independent
  Businesses
Banks
British Franchise Association
BSI Standards
Business in the Community
Business Link
Confederation of British Industry
  (CBI)
Chambers of Commerce
Chartered Institute of Marketing
Companies House
Conferences
Contributions Agency
Council for Small Industries in
  Rural Areas
Customs and Excise
Data Protection Registrar
Department of the Environment
Department of Social Security
Department of Trade and Industry
DTI Loan Guarantee Section
Dun and Bradstreet

Education Colleges
Enterprise Agencies
Exhibitions
Federation of Small Businesses
Forum of Private Business
Health & Safety Executive
Inland Revenue
Institute of Business Counsellors
Institute of Directors
Institute of Personnel &
  Development
Institute of Public Relations
Institute of Sales Promotion
Institute of Trading Standards
Job Centres
Law Society
Libraries
Livewire
Local Authorities
National Federation of Self
  Employed and Small Businesses
National Market Traders'
  Federation
Office of Data Protection
Office of Fair Trading
Open University
OwnBase
Patent Office
Prince's Youth Business Trust
Small Business Bureau
Small Firms Information Service
Solicitors

TECs
Tourist Boards
Trade Associations
Wyvern Business Library
Yellow Pages
Youth Enterprise Service

Possible Suitable Businesses

Set out here are a list of businesses which could be run through a limited company. The list is by no means exhaustive but does give an idea of the types of business which may be suitable.

Advertising agency
Agricultural machinery
Air conditioning
Alarm systems
Audio visual equipment
Bathroom equipment
Bedroom fitters
Beer distributors
Boiler engineers
Brewers
Builders' merchants
Bus hire
Canteen equipment
Car accessories
Car dealers
Catering products
Coachbuilders
Computer consumables
Copying equipment

Crane hire
Dance halls
Data storage
Department store
Display fitters
DIY
Double glazing
Electrical appliances
Engine manufacturers
Entertainment agencies
Exhibition organisers
Factory cleaners
Fencing manufacturers
Fish farms
Food processors
Fuel distributors
Furniture storage
Garage services
Garden centres
Gas installers
Glass manufacturers
Golf equipment
Hardware
Heating equipment
Horticultural equipment
Hotels
House builders
Hygiene services
Independent financial advisers
Insurance brokers
Jewellers
Joinery manufacturers

Kitchen equipment
Laundries
Leasing companies
Loft insulation
Machinery dealers
Management consultants
Metal finishers
Motels
Music systems
Neon signs
Nursery equipment
Nursing homes
Office equipment hire
Office furniture
Oil distribution
Packaging machinery
Pawnbrokers
Pig breeders
Plant hire
Printers
Publishers
Quarries
Refrigeration engineers
Retirement homes
Road contractors
Safety equipment
Scaffolding hire
Spraying equipment
Steel fabricators
Telecommunications
Travel agents
Truck rental

Tyre dealers
Ventilation equipment
Waste disposal
Windscreen services
Yacht chandlers
Zinc metal work

or anything else you wish.
There are many more.

Index